SMART GUIDE

CREATIVE HOMEOWNER®

ceramic tile

step-by-step projects

CREATIVE HOMEOWNER®, Upper Saddle River, New Jersey

CREATIVE HOMEOWNER®
A Division of Federal Marketing Corp.
Upper Saddle River, NJ

Manufactured in the United States of America

Editorial Director: Timothy O. Bakke
Production Manager: Kimberly H. Vivas

Writer: Jim Barrett
Editors: Kimberly Kerrigone, Fran Donegan
Photo Researcher: Sharon Ranftle
Project Assistant: Mindy Circelli

Senior Graphic Designer: David Geer
Graphic Designer: Annie Jeon
Illustrators: James Randolph, Norman Nuding
Cover: John Parsekian (photography), Clarke Barre (design)

Current Printing (last digit)
10 9 8 7 6

Smart Guide: Ceramic Tile
Library of Congress Control Number: 2002104992
ISBN:1-58011-103-3

CREATIVE HOMEOWNER®
A Division of Federal Marketing Corp.
24 Park Way
Upper Saddle River, NJ 07458
www.creativehomeowner.com

Photo Credits

page 1: Tony Giammarino **page 3:** *all* Association of Italian Ceramic Tile and Refractories Manufacturers (ASSOPIASTRELLE) **page 5:** *top left, top right, & left center* Dal-Tile Intl.; *bottom row* ASSOPIASTRELLE **page 9:** *all* John Parsekian **page 19:** *top left* Holly Stickley; *right* Dal-Tile Intl.; *bottom left* Florida Tile **page 39:** *top left & top right* American Olean; *bottom row* ASSOPIASTRELLE **page 55:** *all* Dal-Tile Intl. **page 67:** *top left* Mark Lohman; *top center* Dal-Tile Intl.; *top right* ASSOPIASTRELLE; *bottom* Jessie Walker **page 71:** *top left* Dal-Tile Intl.; *top right* Holly Stickley; *bottom right* Nancy Hill; *bottom left* Tim Street-Porter/Beateworks.com

Metric Conversion

Length

1 inch	25.4 mm
1 foot	0.3048 m
1 yard	0.9144 m
1 mile	1.61 km

Area

1 square inch	645 mm^2
1 square foot	0.0929 m^2
1 square yard	0.8361 m^2
1 acre	4046.86 m^2
1 square mile	2.59 km^2

Volume

1 cubic inch	16.3870 cm^3
1 cubic foot	0.03 m^3
1 cubic yard	0.77 m^3

Common Lumber Equivalents

Sizes: Metric cross sections are so close to their U.S. sizes, as noted below, that for most purposes they may be considered equivalents.

Dimensional lumber	1 × 2	19 × 38 mm
	1 × 4	19 × 89 mm
	2 × 2	38 × 38 mm
	2 × 4	38 × 89 mm
	2 × 6	38 × 140 mm
	2 × 8	38 × 184 mm
	2 × 10	38 × 235 mm
	2 × 12	38 × 286 mm

Capacity

1 fluid ounce	29.57 mL
1 pint	473.18 mL
1 quart	1.14 L
1 gallon	3.79 L

Weight

1 ounce	28.35g
1 pound	0.45kg

Temperature

Fahrenheit = Celsius × 1.8 + 32
Celsius = Fahrenheit – 32 × 5⁄9

Nail Size & Length

Penny Size	Nail Length
2d	1"
3d	1¼"
4d	1½"
5d	1¾"
6d	2"
7d	2¼"
8d	2½"
9d	2¾"
10d	3"
12d	3¼"
16d	3½"

contents

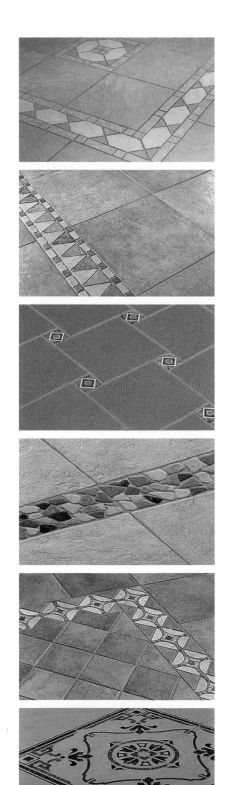

safety first

Though all the designs and methods in this book have been reviewed for safety, it is not possible to overstate the importance of using the safest construction methods possible. What follows are reminders; some do's and don'ts of basic carpentry. They are not substitutes for your own common sense.

- *Always* use caution, care, and good judgment when following the procedures described in this book.

- *Always* be sure that the electrical setup is safe; be sure that no circuit is overloaded and that all power tools and electrical outlets are properly grounded. Do not use power tools in wet locations.

- *Always* read container labels on paints, solvents, and other products; provide ventilation, and observe all other warnings.

- *Always* read the manufacturer's instructions for using a tool, especially the warnings.

- *Always* use hold-downs and push sticks whenever possible when working on a table saw. Avoid working short pieces if you can.

- *Always* remove the key from any drill chuck (portable or press) before starting the drill.

- *Always* pay deliberate attention to how a tool works so that you can avoid being injured.

- *Always* know the limitations of your tools. Do not try to force them to do what they were not designed to do.

- *Always* make sure that any adjustment is locked before proceeding. For example, always check the rip fence on a table saw or the bevel adjustment on a portable saw before starting to work.

- *Always* clamp small pieces firmly to a bench or other work surface when using a power tool on them.

- *Always* wear the appropriate rubber or work gloves when handling chemicals, moving or stacking lumber, or doing heavy construction.

- *Always* wear a disposable face mask when you create dust by sawing or sanding. Use a special filtering respirator when working with toxic substances and solvents.

- *Always* wear eye protection, especially when using power tools or striking metal on metal or concrete; a chip can fly off, for example, when chiseling concrete.

- *Always* be aware that there is seldom enough time for your body's reflexes to save you from injury from a power tool in a dangerous situation; everything happens too fast. Be *alert!*

- *Always* keep your hands away from the business ends of blades, cutters, and bits.

- *Always* hold a circular saw firmly, usually with both hands so that you know where they are.

- *Always* use a drill with an auxiliary handle to control the torque when large-size bits are used.

- *Always* check your local building codes when planning new construction. The codes are intended to protect public safety and should be observed to the letter.

- *Never* work with power tools when you are tired or under the influence of alcohol or drugs.

- *Never* cut tiny pieces of wood or pipe using a power saw. Cut small pieces off larger pieces.

- *Never* change a saw blade or a drill or router bit unless the power cord is unplugged. Do not depend on the switch being off; you might accidentally hit it.

- *Never* work in insufficient lighting.

- *Never* work while wearing loose clothing, hanging hair, open cuffs, or jewelry.

- *Never* work with dull tools. Have them sharpened, or learn how to sharpen them yourself.

- *Never* use a power tool on a work-piece—large or small—that is not firmly supported.

- *Never* saw a workpiece that spans a large distance between horses without close support on each side of the cut; the piece can bend, closing on and jamming the blade, causing saw kickback.

- *Never* support a workpiece from underneath with your leg or other part of your body when sawing.

- *Never* carry sharp or pointed tools, such as utility knives, awls, or chisels, in your pocket. If you want to carry such tools, use a special-purpose tool belt with leather pockets and holders.

chapter 1

tile options

Types of Ceramic Tile

Glazed or Unglazed?

Ceramic tile is categorized many different ways. At the most basic level, tiles come either glazed or unglazed. With unglazed tile, the color runs throughout the tile body. The color can be the natural earth tone of the clay itself, or the color of a pigment that has been added to it before firing. Glazed tiles, on the other hand, have color which has been added to the surface of the tile. The color is applied to the tile after firing. The tile is then fired again to bond the glaze to the clay body. Glazed tiles range from a high gloss to a dull matte finish, and come in a much wider range of colors, patterns and surface textures.

Water Absorption

The tile body itself (called bisque) is classified by its porosity (the amount of water it will absorb). Nonvitreous tile absorbs 7 percent or more water; semivitreous tile absorbs between 3 percent and 7 percent water; vitreous tile absorbs between 0.5 percent and 3 percent water, and impervious tile absorbs less than 0.5 percent water. Nonvitreous tiles include porous white-bodied, glazed wall tiles and low-fired, porous, red-bodied patio tiles and handmade pavers. At the other end of the spectrum, vitreous and impervious tiles include ceramic and glass mosaic tiles and porcelain tiles.

While the glazed surface of any tile is impervious to water, glazed tiles are not necessarily more water-resistant than those that are unglazed. If the glazed surface is scratched or abraded, water will penetrate into the tile body. Water can also enter through grout joints between the tiles. Tile density or porosity becomes important when choosing tiles for wet conditions (such as in a bathroom or on a kitchen countertop), because water absorbed by porous tiles can harbor bacteria and will eventually penetrate through the tile to the substrate, loosening the adhesive bond. While tile dealers generally do not group tiles by porosity, this information is usually available if you ask for it.

Glazed Wall Tiles

This type of tile is available in a wide variety of sizes, colors and patterns. Most custom decorative and hand-painted tiles fall into this category. Typically, wall tiles are thin, light-weight, nonvitreous tiles coated with a soft, fragile glaze, making them unsuitable for floors. Some wall tiles can also be used for countertops and backsplashes while others cannot. Similarly, some are suitable for wet areas, such as a tub surround or shower enclosure, depending on the porosity of the tile body and the durability of the glaze used. For such applications, you usually will need to apply a waterproofing sealer to protect the grout joints against water penetration. While many tile catalogs do not identify wall tiles in this way, they do specify the surfaces and conditions for which a particular tile is suitable.

Wall tiles are typically ¼ inch to ⅜ inch thick, and range in size from 3x3 inches to 6x6 inches square, although you may find them in larger sizes and different shapes.

Sheet-Mounted Tiles

These consist of evenly spaced wall tiles mounted on a backing sheet of paper, plastic or fabric mesh, or a silicone tab grid. Sheet sizes are 12 inches square or larger, and may contain anywhere from 8 to 64 tiles. While sheet-mounted wall tiles eliminate the laborious process of spacing individual tiles, they are often more expensive per square foot than individual tiles of comparable quality. Sizes, colors and surface textures are limited. Some sheet-mounted tiles also can be used on floors and countertops.

Pregrouted Tile Panels

These tiles take sheet tiles a step further by eliminating the need to grout the joints. The "grout" is actually a flexible silicone caulk, which requires no sealing and less maintenance than ordinary grout. The sheets are flexible enough to bend and stretch with normal building movement, and a variety of trim pieces are available to complete the installation. Tubes of matching silicone caulk are used to grout the joints between panel edges and trim pieces. The silicone grout contains a mildew and fungus inhibitor, making these panels suitable for shower and tub enclosures. Conversely, because

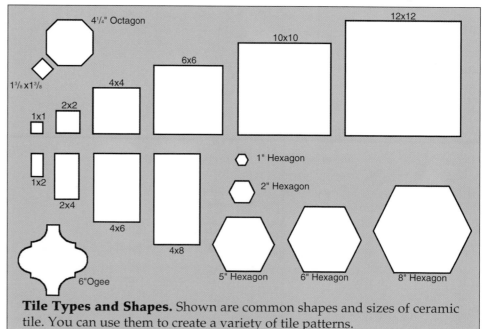

Tile Types and Shapes. Shown are common shapes and sizes of ceramic tile. You can use them to create a variety of tile patterns.

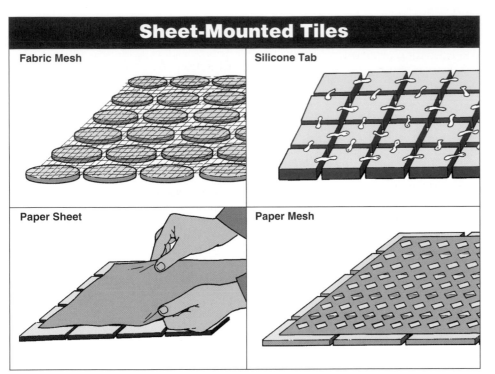

Sheet-Mounted Tiles

Fabric Mesh

Silicone Tab

Paper Sheet

Paper Mesh

of this chemical treatment, the FDA does not recommend installing such sheets on kitchen countertops.

Floor Tiles

Floor tiles are usually thicker than wall tiles—from ½ inch to ¾ inch thick. Sizes for square tiles range from 4 inches to 24 inches square; shapes include rectangular, hexagonal, octagonal, and ogee. Most floor tiles are too heavy to install on walls, although you can do so if you provide adequate structural support and use the right adhesive.

Floor tiles fall into three general categories: unglazed quarry tile, unglazed pavers, and glazed floor tile.

Unglazed Quarry Tiles. This type of tile is a hard-bodied semivitreous or vitreous tile used for indoor and outdoor floors. The bisque is usually a deep, brick red, although other earth tone colors are available.

Pavers. This group includes all unglazed floor tiles that are not classified as quarry tiles. These range from highly vitreous machine-made pavers to soft-bodied, nonvitreous handmade "Mexican" and "patio" tiles. Unglazed pavers and quarry

tiles must be sealed when used on interior floors, to resist dirt and stains. Some sealers also provide a low sheen to the tiles and enhance their natural color. Because the sealers generally are not recommended for use on food preparation areas, and unglazed tiles stain easily, they are not recommended for countertops.

Glazed Tiles. These floor tiles are often listed in manufacturer's catalogs as glazed quarry tile or glazed pavers. Colors range from muted earth tones to bold, bright, solid-color and patterned tiles. Because tile glazes tend to be slick, most glazed floor tiles have a rough or textured surface to make them slip-resistant. Glazed floor tiles also are a good choice for kitchen countertops, tables, and other surfaces subject to frequent use.

Ceramic Mosaic Tile

Any tile 2 inches square or smaller is called ceramic mosaic tile. These tiles are made either of glass, or a fine-grained porcelain clay, mixed with colored pigments. Since they are dense-bodied vitreous tiles, they resist water, stains, impact, and abrasion, making them suitable for

practically any application, indoors or out. Surface textures range from a smooth, glassy surface for walls and countertops to a textured slip-resistant surface for use on floors. Shapes include squares, rectangles, hexagons, circles, teardrops, cloverleafs, or random "pebble" shapes, among others. Most mosaic tiles are mounted on a backing sheet of rubber, plastic, paper or heavy thread, to facilitate application. Because of their small size, these tiles adapt well to contoured or irregular surfaces.

Cement-Bodied Tiles

As the name suggests, these tiles are formed from cement, rather than clay. There are two basic kinds: Mexican saltillo tiles and extruded cement-bodied tiles.

Both saltillo and extruded cement-bodied tiles come in most standard "floor tile" sizes, although shapes are limited to squares and rectangles.

Saltillo Tiles. These tiles, pronounced sal-tee´-yo, are composed of soft clay and are cured by being allowed to simply dry in the sun. The term "saltillo" comes from the salty looking crust that forms on the tile surface, caused by lime leaching from the mortar during and after curing. These tiles come stained in a variety of earth tone colors. Because of their porosity, saltillo tiles require a sealer to help resist staining; for the same reason, they are not suitable for wet locations indoors.

Extruded Cement-Bodied Tiles. This type of tile is made of a mixture of Portland cement, sand, and a fine aggregate (gravel) which is extruded under pressure, then steam-cured in a kiln to produce an extremely dense-bodied tile with good resistance to wear and water absorption. The tiles come in a variety of stained colors, which run throughout the tile body. Tiles intended for indoor use are factory-treated with a clear acrylic surface sealer (rather than an applied glaze like ceramic tile) to give them a semigloss appearance.

Trim Tiles

The standard unit of ceramic tile used to cover a surface is called a field tile. All tiles that are not field tiles are referred to as trim tiles. They are used to create smooth, finished edges and corners for specific areas. In tile catalogs, manufacturers usually picture the available sizes and shapes of trim pieces for different tiles in their line.

Angles. (Left-out, right-out, left-in, right-in). These trim tiles create sharp corners instead of rounded ones.

Apron. Half-size tiles called aprons are used to fill in narrow areas, such as along the front of a countertop.

Beads. Also called quarter-round, this trim is used to finish corners and edges. The pieces are narrow, and they turn a rounded 90-degree angle.

Bullnose. Bullnose trim is a regular field tile with one curved, finished edge. It finishes a course without turning a corner. Often it is paired with an apron tile; the apron tile meets the bullnose at a right angle. The result is a smoothly turned corner and edge.

Countertop Trim or Sink Cap. This special trim piece is set on the outside edge of a countertop. Its raised lip is designed to prevent drips.

Cove. Cove pieces are used to turn corners at a right angle. The corners can turn either inward or outward. Cove base turns a corner at floor level; cove itself turns a corner in any course. Some pieces have a finished edge for turning corners at the top row of a backsplash, for instance. The inside surface of cove is hollow, and therefore compensates for out-of-plumb corners.

Miter. Two miter pieces together in a corner create the look of a miter joint.

Rounds. (In- and out-corner). This trim tile creates a rounded corner instead of an angular one.

Swimming Pool Edging. Designed to cover the coping on swimming pools, this edging requires a thick-set mortar bed.

Window Sill. This tile has a finished edge on one side, and a rounded corner on the other. It covers the sill itself and turns to meet the tile on the wall. Without this trim piece, two tiles are needed—a flat field tile for the sill itself and a quarter-round to turn the corner.

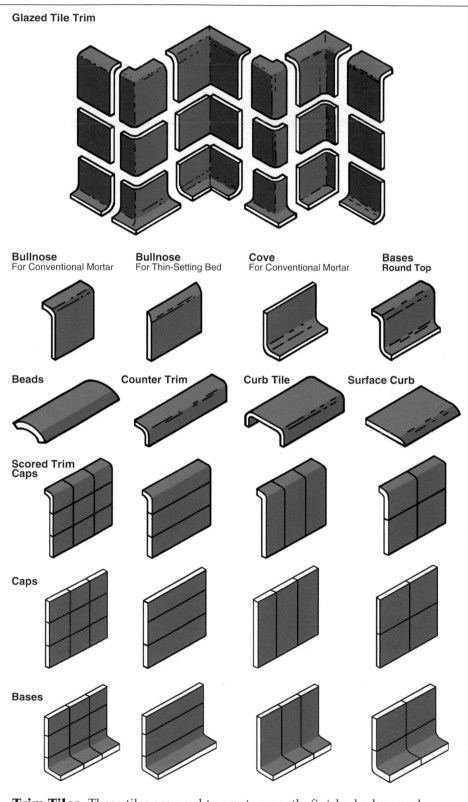

Glazed Tile Trim

| Bullnose For Conventional Mortar | Bullnose For Thin-Setting Bed | Cove For Conventional Mortar | Bases Round Top |

Beads Counter Trim Curb Tile Surface Curb

Scored Trim Caps

Caps

Bases

Trim Tiles. These tiles are used to create smooth, finished edges and corners for specific areas.

chapter 2

what you'll need

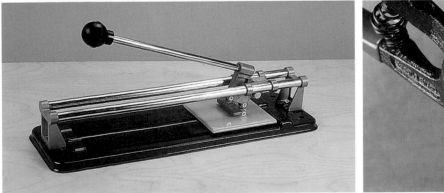

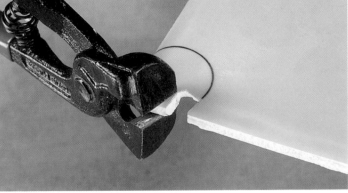

Tiling Tools

If you are an active do-it-yourselfer, you probably already have most of the tools you will need to complete a tile job. If you have a small amount of tiles to cut, you can use an ordinary glass cutter (see next page) but the job will be accomplished faster with a snap cutter. Other required tools include a straightedge, scraper or putty knife, caulking gun, squeegee, and hammer or rubber mallet. Keep several damp sponges and rags handy for cleaning up as you go.

If the surface you are tiling requires more than a little preparation, you may need additional masonry and carpentry tools. Because surface preparation can involve anything from simple cleaning with a sponge and household cleaner to completely rebuilding a wall or floor, specific surface preparation tools will be listed at the start of projects in which they are required.

You can buy most of the specialized tile-setting tools you will need at a local hardware store, home center or tile dealer. Expensive items, such as a snap-cutter or wet saw, can be rented from the tile dealer or a tool-rental shop. (Many tile dealers will loan you the tools you need if you buy your tiles and other supplies from them.)

Layout Tools. This group includes a 2-foot level, steel tape measure, 2-foot carpenter's square, combination square, plumb bob, and chalkline.

Another handy layout tool called a layout stick is one you can make yourself. It is a stick that has been marked in increments of tile and grout-joint widths. You can make the stick as long as you need—from 6 to 10 "tiles" long or longer. After marking the stick, use it to transfer the measurements to the surface being tiled. It also can be used to quickly estimate the number of tiles needed to cover a particular area.

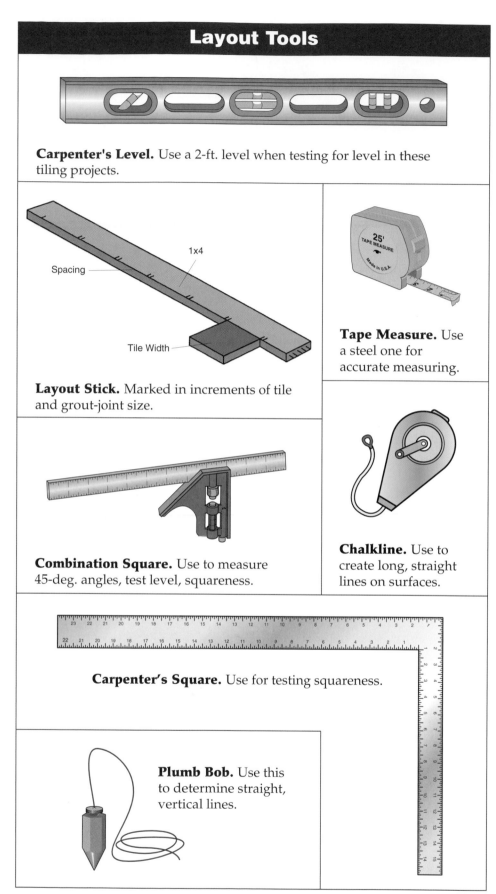

Layout Tools

Carpenter's Level. Use a 2-ft. level when testing for level in these tiling projects.

Layout Stick. Marked in increments of tile and grout-joint size.

Spacing · 1x4 · Tile Width

Tape Measure. Use a steel one for accurate measuring.

Combination Square. Use to measure 45-deg. angles, test level, squareness.

Chalkline. Use to create long, straight lines on surfaces.

Carpenter's Square. Use for testing squareness.

Plumb Bob. Use this to determine straight, vertical lines.

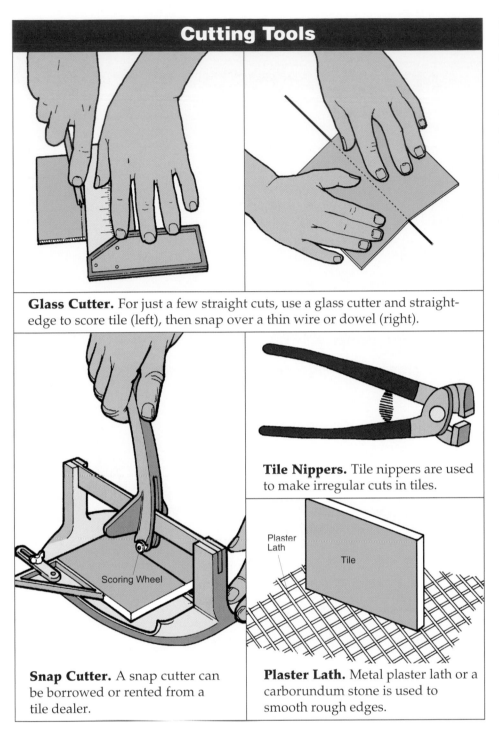

Cutting Tools

Glass Cutter. For just a few straight cuts, use a glass cutter and straightedge to score tile (left), then snap over a thin wire or dowel (right).

Snap Cutter. A snap cutter can be borrowed or rented from a tile dealer.

Tile Nippers. Tile nippers are used to make irregular cuts in tiles.

Plaster Lath. Metal plaster lath or a carborundum stone is used to smooth rough edges.

Cutting Tools. To make straight cuts in most glazed tile, all you need is a conventional glass cutter, a short metal straightedge or square, and a short length of coat-hanger wire. Simply score the glazed surface of the tile with the cutter and straightedge, then place the tile on the wire with the score mark centered directly above it. Press down on both sides of the tile to snap it.

If you have many straight cuts to make, a snap cutter (available at tool-rental shops) will speed things along considerably. After positioning the tile in the cutter, draw the carbide blade or wheel lightly across the tile

to score it, then press down on the handle to snap the tile. Some snapcutters may not work on very large, thick tiles.

If you have just a few large tiles to cut, use this variation of the score-and-snap method: Equip a hacksaw with a carbide-grit blade, then cut a groove about $\frac{1}{16}$ inch deep in the face of the tile (very thick tiles may require a second cut on the backside to get a clean snap). Place the tile over a wood dowel or length of heavy insulated wire and press down sharply to snap the tile. A carborundum stone or whetstone comes in handy for smoothing rough tile edges; you can also use a piece of metal plaster lath. If you have many large tiles to cut, use a wet saw.

A wet saw is used to make clean, smooth, straight cuts in all types of tile. It can also be used to make cutouts in the edges of tile. To do this, make a series of parallel cuts inside the area to be removed, then snap off the pieces with tile nippers. Most tile dealers have a wet saw, and will make cuts for a small fee. You also can rent one at a tool rental shop.

Tile nippers or biters are used to make curved or irregularly shaped cuts in the edges of tiles, such as when fitting tiles around supply pipes, sink cutouts, or other obstructions. As the name implies, you use this plier-type tool to nip away tiny bits of tile within the cutout area until the desired shape is achieved. To use the nippers, hold the tile with the glazed side up and take small, $\frac{1}{8}$-inch bites to break off tiny pieces at a time.

Because ceramic tile is brittle, none of the above cutting tools work 100 percent of the time: Make sure you buy enough extra tiles to allow for breakage and other mistakes. If you do not want to cut tiles at all, you can carefully lay out all the tiles in advance, mark the ones that need to be cut, and have the tile dealer cut them for you.

Setting Tools. This group includes tools for mixing and spreading tile adhesive or mortar, a rubber mallet or hammer, and a bedding block to level and seat the tiles in the adhesive. You will also need a straightedge to assure that the tiles are level with one another, and some method of spacing the tiles to establish the grout joints.

In most cases, a notched trowel is all you will need to apply the adhesive. Typically, only one side and one end of the trowel is notched. The flat side is used to spread the adhesive evenly on the substrate, and the notched side is used to comb evenly spaced ridges in the adhesive. These trowels come with various sized square or V-shaped notches for spreading different types of adhesives with different types of tiles. The required notch size is usually specified in literature provided by the tile or adhesive manufacturer.

Organic adhesives and some thinset cement-based adhesives are available premixed. Traditional thick-set cement mortar, most thinset adhesives, and two-part epoxy adhesives will require mixing. For mixing very large amounts of cement-based adhesives, you will need a shovel, hoe and wheelbarrow, as you would for mixing concrete. For mixing smaller amounts of mortar, thinset adhesives or powdered grout (2 to 10 gallons), you can use a bucket or large plastic tray and a heavy stick or a paint mixer chucked in a heavy-duty electric drill. Very small amounts of these materials (less than about 2 gallons) can be hand-mixed with an ordinary paint stick, large mixing spoon, putty knife, or similar tool, in a small plastic bucket or paint tray. Various other mason's tools, such as floats and trowels, will be needed to level and finish thickset mortar beds (a job best left to a professional).

To bed the tiles firmly into the adhesive, you will need a rubber mallet (for smaller tiles) or a hammer and bedding block (for larger tiles). To make a bedding block, cut a wood block large enough to cover several tiles at once. Then cover it with a piece of felt, heavy fabric or scrap carpet. To use the bedding block, slide it across the tiles while tapping it lightly with a hammer to bed the tiles firmly in the adhesive. During this process, you will also need a metal straightedge or carpenter's square to periodically check the tiles. Make sure they are even and level, and that the grout joints between remain in alignment.

Setting Tools

Notched Trowel. The smooth side of a notched trowel is used to apply adhesive; the notched side combs ridges of correct depth to adhere the tile.

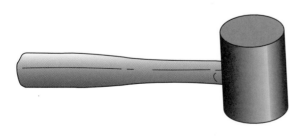

Rubber Mallet. Use a rubber mallet or hammer to tap the bedding block.

Bedding Block. Use a carpet-covered length of 2x4 to bed the tile into the adhesive.

Spacers. When setting individual ceramic tiles, allow space between them for grout joints. To assure even, uniform spacing for grout joints, some tiles (typically wall tiles) have built-in spacers (nubs) molded into the sides of each unit.

If the tiles you are using do not have such spacers, you can buy molded plastic spacers from a tile dealer. These small plastic crosses come in various sizes for creating grout joints from $\frac{1}{32}$ inch to $\frac{1}{2}$ inch wide. Some types can be removed and reused (once the tile "grabs" in the adhesive, but before the adhesive cures completely). Others can be left in place and grouted over.

If you do not want to incur the extra cost of manufactured spacers, or cannot find any in the width you want, you can use cotton cord or rope, toothpicks, matchsticks, nails, dowels, plywood strips or similar items as spacers. All of these are removed before the adhesive sets.

One way to space tiles on walls or countertops is to mark the centers of the grout lines (in both directions) on the surface to be tiled. Then, attach 6d finishing nails at each end of the prospective grout lines, and stretch pieces of dampened cotton cord or rope between them to serve as spacers, and install the tiles along the lines. After aligning the tiles in one direction, remove the cords and nails. Then reposition them to establish the perpendicular joints.

On floors and other surfaces with wider grout joints, small wood spacers combined with wood battens can be used.

Spacers

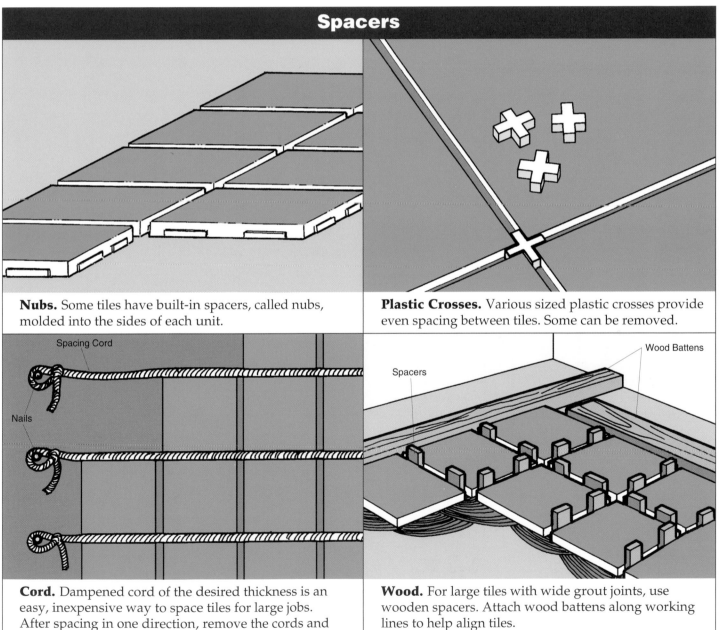

Nubs. Some tiles have built-in spacers, called nubs, molded into the sides of each unit.

Plastic Crosses. Various sized plastic crosses provide even spacing between tiles. Some can be removed.

Spacing Cord

Nails

Cord. Dampened cord of the desired thickness is an easy, inexpensive way to space tiles for large jobs. After spacing in one direction, remove the cords and reconnect them at right angles.

Wood Battens

Spacers

Wood. For large tiles with wide grout joints, use wooden spacers. Attach wood battens along working lines to help align tiles.

Grouting and Sealing Tools.
Unglazed tiles often are sealed before and after grouting to protect the grout joints. To properly apply a clear sealant, use a clean foam-rubber roller.

Grout is usually applied by spreading a liberal amount across the tile surface and forcing it into the joints with a rubber float or squeegee, then wiping off the excess with the same tool.

A grout bag (similar to a pastry bag) is another option for applying grout. These bags have a small fitting on one end to which different size nozzles can be attached to control the amount of grout applied to the joint. Fill the bag with grout. Then, squeeze the bag to lay a bead of grout directly into the joint. Grout bags work well in situations where cleaning excess grout off the tile surface would be difficult, or where the grout might stain the tile surface, such as when using colored grouts with unglazed quarry tiles or pavers. Using a bag, however, does have a couple of drawbacks. First, the grout must be mixed to a consistency that enables you to squeeze it from the bag, which might make it too thin or watery to achieve adequate strength. It may be difficult to apply fast-setting grouts using this method. Second, using a grout bag is time consuming; it's much faster and easier to pour the grout directly from the mixing container and to squeegee it into the joints.

After the grout has been applied, and most of the excess has been removed, clean the tiles with a damp sponge, rinsing frequently.

Special striking tools are available for shaping or "striking" the grout joints after the grout is applied, but they are not essential. Items such as dowels, spoons, toothbrush handles, or even shaped wooden sticks make effective striking tools. A mildew-resistant silicone tub-and-tile caulk is usually used to fill gaps or joints where tile meets surfaces of dissimilar materials, such as where a tile floor meets the wall, or where the tile abuts fixtures such as a tub, shower pan or sink. While you can buy silicone caulk in small squeeze tubes, it is neater and more economical to buy it in cartridges and apply it with a caulking gun.

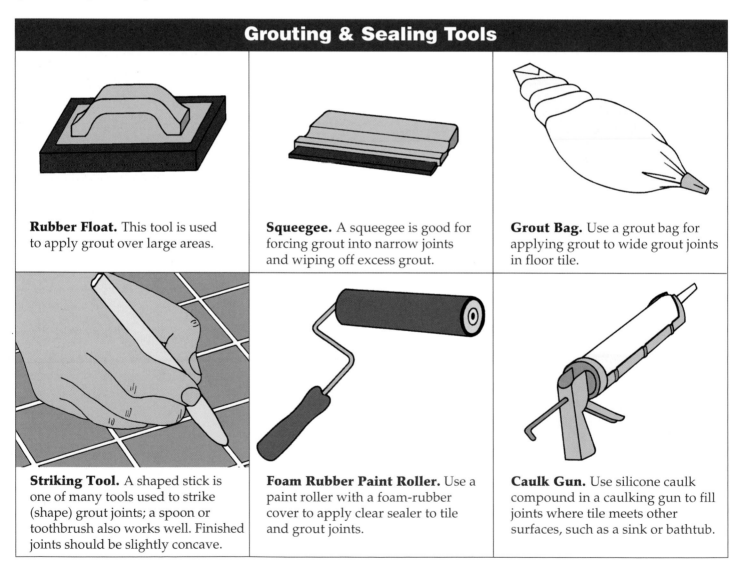

Grouting & Sealing Tools

Rubber Float. This tool is used to apply grout over large areas.

Squeegee. A squeegee is good for forcing grout into narrow joints and wiping off excess grout.

Grout Bag. Use a grout bag for applying grout to wide grout joints in floor tile.

Striking Tool. A shaped stick is one of many tools used to strike (shape) grout joints; a spoon or toothbrush also works well. Finished joints should be slightly concave.

Foam Rubber Paint Roller. Use a paint roller with a foam-rubber cover to apply clear sealer to tile and grout joints.

Caulk Gun. Use silicone caulk compound in a caulking gun to fill joints where tile meets other surfaces, such as a sink or bathtub.

Mortar & Adhesives

The traditional method of setting ceramic tile, called "thick-bed" installation, involves laying the tiles directly in a bed of wet portland cement mortar. While some professional tile-setters still use this method today, the development of "thinset" mortars and organic mastics have made it possible to easily install tiles directly over a variety of surfaces. The traditional thick-bed mortar base has its advantages, such as leveling an uneven floor, or providing a slope for drainage in a shower.

Thick-Bed. Because it is unaffected by water, thick-bed installations have long been the preferred method for installing tile in wet areas, such as tub and shower enclosures. However installing thick-bed mortar requires considerable experience and a variety of tools to do the job correctly, especially when the job requires installing it on walls. Typically, the tiles must be soaked in water before setting them in this type of bed. When a thick-bed installation is required, most tile-setters will lay down the mortar bed, smooth it,

allow it to cure, and then set the tiles over the bed with a "bond coat" of thinset cement adhesive. In either case, the procedure is best left to a professional and therefore is not covered in this book.

Thinset. Thin-bed or thinset adhesives have made it possible for practically anyone to complete a successful tile job. However, you will find a bewildering variety of these adhesives on the market. There are not only different types of adhesives

for various applications, but also many different brands on the market that vary in price and quality. A reputable tile dealer can recommend the best adhesive for the job, but it helps to have a basic knowledge of how adhesives are categorized and the uses for each type. All tile-setting adhesives fall into three basic categories: cement-based thinset adhesives (mortars), organic adhesives (mastics), and epoxy-based adhesives.

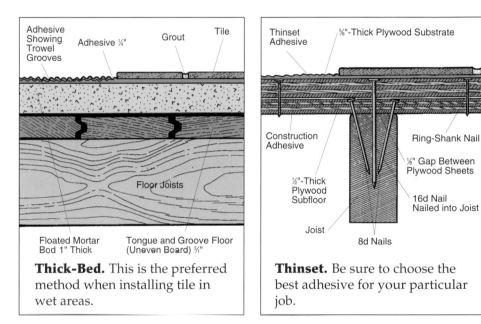

Thick-Bed. This is the preferred method when installing tile in wet areas.

Thinset. Be sure to choose the best adhesive for your particular job.

Safety Equipment & Procedures

As with any remodeling job, setting tile involves certain hazards, both physical and chemical. When using any tool to cut tile, wear safety glasses or goggles to protect your eyes from flying chips of material. Also wear goggles when working with any power tool and when doing related jobs such as knocking down walls. Because cut tile edges can be sharp, wear heavy leather or canvas gloves when handling them.

Most cutting, sanding, and grinding procedures create dust,

which can irritate your lungs. Many building materials, including some resilient and ceramic tiles, contain asbestos and other carcinogens. Breathing the dust puts your health at risk, so it is wise to wear a respirator when working with any building materials. For specific safety procedures related to removing resilient floorcoverings, see page 23.

Dust from powdered grouts also may contain toxic substances. A fitted rubber mask with replaceable cartridges provides much

more protection than a flimsy paper or fabric dust mask. You also can fit the rubber mask with cartridges that filter out harmful chemical fumes associated with some organic adhesives, epoxies, grouts, sealers, and similar products. Some of these products irritate the skin, so wear chemical-resistant rubber gloves when working with them. Always read and follow label precautions for the materials you are using. For additional tips on safe construction practices, see page 4.

Cement-Based Adhesives. These are actually forms of cement-based mortar, although they should not be confused with the portland cement mortar used for thick-bed installations. Most of these nonflammable thinset mortars come in powder form (some must be mixed with sand before use while others come presanded). Some are available in ready-to-use, premixed liquid form. Powdered forms must be mixed with water, liquid latex or acrylic solution.

Dry-set mortars are thinset adhesives, consisting of cement combined with additives to retard the curing process. Most come in a powder form and are mixed with water. They are called dry-set because even though they have a cement base, there is no need to presoak the tiles, as for thick-bed installation. Highly resistant to impact, dry-set mortar is easily cleaned with water. Once cured, it is not affected by prolonged contact with water, so it can be used in wet installations, such as bathroom floors. An appropriate waterproof membrane or backing material should be installed ahead of time to prevent water penetration into the substrate material underneath.

A ³⁄₃₂-inch thick layer of dry-set mortar will cover and level minor surface irregularities, but it is not intended as a setting bed or for leveling very rough surfaces. Dry-set mortars adhere well to a variety of substrate materials, including relatively smooth, plumb masonry and concrete, Styrofoam, insulation board, drywall, tile backer board, cured portland cement beds, ceramic tile and stone. Some types are suitable for use over plywood.

Latex-portland cement mortars are a mixture of portland cement, sand, and a liquid latex or acrylic additive. These thinset mortars have many of the same applications as water-soluble dry-set mortars, plus a few more. Generally they have a higher compressive and bond strength than

dry-set, and are more flexible and water-resistant. While latex portland cement mortars cost a bit more than dry-set, they are generally superior in quality.

Organic Mastic Adhesives. Simply called mastics, organic adhesives come in a ready-to-use premixed paste form. They cure or set by evaporation. While most of these adhesives do not have the bond strength or leveling properties of thinsets, they are the easiest for do-it-yourselfers to apply. There are two drawbacks to using organic mastics. They must be applied to relatively smooth, level backings, and most brands cannot be used for wet installations. Suitable backings include drywall, smooth plaster or mortar, plywood, tile backer board, and smooth, dry concrete. Some brands can be applied to plastic laminates or existing ceramic tile.

Organic mastics are either solvent-based or water-based, and are referred to as Type I and Type II mastics respectively. Solvent-based Type I mastics contain petroleum ditillates (typically toulene) and generally provide more water resistance than latex-based Type II mastics. Type I mastics are highly flammable and should be used in a well-ventilated area, away from sparks or flame. A respirator with the appropriate cartridge should be worn as the fumes are poisonous. Type II mastics are somewhat safer to use, but precautions should be taken to provide sufficient ventilation and gloves should be worn to avoid skin contact.

You will find numerous brands and formulas of these type of mastics. Generally, they are specified either for use on floors or on walls . Most cannot be used in areas subject to heat, such as fireplace hearths or wood stove surrounds. Check label instructions for specific applications.

Epoxy-Based Mortars. Also called epoxies, this group of mortars are not used much by do-it-yourselfers

because they are more expensive and harder to apply than other adhesives. The resin and hardener must be mixed to exact proportions and applied at the correct temperature to ensure the right setting time and pot life. Because epoxy mortars tend to sag, you may have problems when using them on walls and other vertical surfaces.

However, epoxy mortars combined with epoxy grouts provide superior bond strength and excellent resistance to impact and chemicals. Epoxies will adhere to just about any substrate material, including existing ceramic tile, metal, and plywood. Some also are heat resistant, making them a good choice for applications such as range hoods or tiled surrounds for wood stoves or fireplaces. For most situations resort to an epoxy only when the surface being tiled is not compatible with any other adhesive type. Epoxies consist of a resin and hardener, much like the two-part epoxy glues sold at hardware stores (some of these include a filler material). Epoxy mortars are used when a high degree of bond strength is required or when the tiled surface will receive a high degree of physical or chemical wear.

After mixing the adhesive, apply one thin layer. Pot life, adhesion, ability to clean up with water before cure, and chemical resistance vary with different brands, so choose formulations carefully. Epoxies are highly water resistant but not completely waterproof. Like other adhesives, they should be used in conjunction with a surface sealer and a waterproof membrane to protect the substrate in wet conditions.

Similar to epoxy adhesives, furan resin adhesives come as a two-part resin and hardener system, and are used in commercial and industrial situations that require a high degree of chemical resistance. Furan adhesives and grouts are rarely used for residential applications.

Grouts

As with adhesives, recommended formulas for grouts vary depending upon application. All tile grouts fall into two basic categories: cement-based grout and epoxy grout. Grouts used for tiling should not be confused with caulks, which are elastomeric materials used for filling gaps between various building materials.

Commercial Portland-Cement. This mixture of portland cement and other ingredients produces a dense, uniformly colored material. Like cement-based mortars, it is resistant to water, but not completely water-proof or stainproof, so it requires a sealer. Commercial portland-cement grouts are formulated for use with thick-bed portland-cement mortar installations for which the installer must soak the tiles in water for 15 to 20 minutes before application. These grouts also require damp curing (keeping the surface moist until the grout cures) to prevent it from shrinking and cracking. Formulations for walls are usually white while those for floors are gray. Portland-cement grout is available unsanded or presanded. Unsanded grouts typically are used for joints less than $\frac{1}{16}$ inch wide. For joints up to $\frac{1}{8}$ inch wide, a mixture of one part cement to one part 30-mesh sand is used; for joints $\frac{1}{8}$ inch to $\frac{1}{2}$ inch wide, one part cement to 2 parts 30-mesh sand; for joints over $\frac{1}{2}$ inch wide, one part cement to three parts all-purpose sand.

Cement-Based. These grouts all have a base of portland cement, but differ in the types of additives they contain. A variety of precolored grouts are also available. If you use a colored grout, bear in mind that it may stain some unglazed tiles. Most cement-based grouts come in pow-dered form to which water or liquid latex is added. A few are premixed and ready to use, although usually more expensive.

Dry-Set. This type of portland-cement grout contains additives that increase water-retentiveness, enabling you to grout tiles without presoaking them and damp-curing the grout once applied (hence, the name "dry-set"). However, when grouting the tiles on a hot, dry day, the grout might dry out so quickly that it will shrink, requiring the tiles to be presoaked and the grout joints to be damp-cured.

Latex-Portland Cement. Any of the three preceding grout types, can be mixed with liquid latex instead of water. This mixture is the most versatile all-around grout for a variety of residential applications.

Epoxy. Epoxy grout contains a resin and hardener, giving it a high degree of chemical resistance, excellent bond strength, and superior impact resistance. It is the most expensive grout, and therefore usually confined to commercial applications. An epoxy grout would be a good choice for a countertop in which a certain degree of chemical resistance is required. Epoxy grout has a consistency some-what like heavy syrup and is not easy to apply. For example, if the tiles are more than $\frac{1}{2}$ inch thick and the grout joints are less than $\frac{1}{4}$ inch wide, the joint will be too narrow for the grout to fully penetrate.

Silicone. Silicone caulk is used at joints where tile meets other surfaces, but it is also used to grout between tiles in some cases. Pregrouted tile sheets, for instance, have silicone grout joints. They generally come with a tube of matching grout to seal joints where the panels meet. Also, because silicone is highly flexible, it is often used in lieu of grout at tiled corners where movement in the substructure would crack ordinary grout joints, such as where a countertop meets a backsplash.

Sealers

Tile and grout sealers provide protection against stains, and to some extent, water penetration. As a final step in tile installation, they are used for unglazed tiles and grout joints. While glazed tiles do not require a sealer, cement-based grouts usually do. Most sealers have a silicone, lacquer or acrylic base. Different formulations are available for different types of tile and grout in different applications (walls, floors, wet areas, outdoors, etc.). A tile dealer can recommend the appropriate sealer. To maintain protective qualities, sealers require periodic reapplication.

Grout Type

		Commercial Portland Cement Wall Use	Commercial Portland Cement Floor Use	Sand Portland Cement Wall-Floor Use	Dry-set Wall-Floor Use	Latex Portland Cement	Epoxy	Silicone
Tile Type	Glazed Wall	√			√	√		√
	Ceramic Mosaics	√	√	√	√	√	√	√
	Quarry, Paver & Packing House	√	√	√		√	√	
Areas of Use	Dry & Intermittently Wet	√	√	√	√	√	√	√
	Prolonged Wet	√	√	√	√	√	√	√
	Exteriors	√	√	√	√	√	√	

Other Tiling Materials

Beyond adhesives, grouts and sealers, certain tile projects may require special backing materials or other specialized materials for preparing the surface to be tiled.

Tile Backer Board. Also called cementitious backer units, or CBUs, tile backer board is a rigid, portland-cement-based panel used as a backing for ceramic tile in wet or dry areas. Different types are specified for interior floors and walls, and exterior walls. Two common brands are Durock® and Wonderboard®. Backer board is the best substrate to use in wet areas because it is unaffected by water (wood, plywood, particleboard, and drywall underlayments deteriorate when exposed to water). Also, because it is a rigid, dense, dimensionally stable cement-based product, it does not have the expansion and contraction problems associated with conventional wood subflooring and floor underlayment materials.

Backer board is available in ½-inch and ⁵⁄₁₆-inch-thick sheets in standard widths from 32 inches (to fit the end walls above conventional-width bathtubs) to 48 inches, in lengths from 4 feet and 8 feet. Backer board is installed directly over bare wall studs, the same way that drywall is installed. Joints between panels are sealed with a special fiberglass mesh tape and liquid sealer. Because backer board is also fireproof, it makes an excellent insulating material for wood stove surrounds.

Waterproof Membranes. Even when glazed tiles, water-resistant adhesives and grouts, and a waterproofing sealer have been used, water still can seep through these materials and weaken the bond between the tile and substrate, causing damage to the framing underneath. In wet conditions such as a shower or tub surround, waterproof membranes are sometimes installed between the studs and the substrate to prevent such damage. Other typical indoor locations include sunken tubs, bathroom or laundryroom floors, and sink areas in countertops or vanities. Waterproof membranes also work in reverse when installing tile over concrete floors subject to moisture penetration from beneath, such as in a basement. Tar paper or building felt has long been the traditional material used for a waterproofing membrane. Other types of membranes include polyethylene sheeting and combination liquid and fabric membranes. Each has its advantages and drawbacks in various situations. Also, because local building codes and practices vary, as well as individual installations and local environmental conditions, seek the advice of a local architect or building engineer to determine whether or not your installation requires a waterproof membrane. If so, determine which type is appropriate.

Isolation Membranes. Similar to waterproofing membranes, these membranes "isolate" the tile from the underlayment to compensate for different expansion and contraction rates of the dissimilar materials. Isolation membranes are often required when the existing underlayment shows signs of excessive movement, due to seasonal changes in temperature and humidity, or settling of the house. Signs include cracks in plaster or masonry, sagging floors, and cracks at joints where two different subflooring materials meet (such as a concrete slab abutting a wood subfloor). If you do suspect excessive seasonal movement or a weak substructure, we recommend that you seek professional advice.

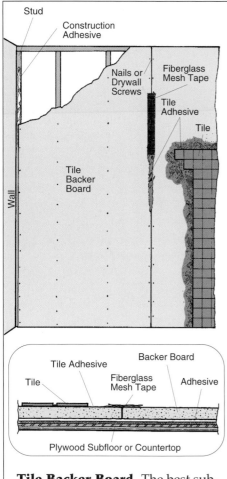

Tile Backer Board. The best substrate for installations, it is smooth, rigid, and unaffected by water.

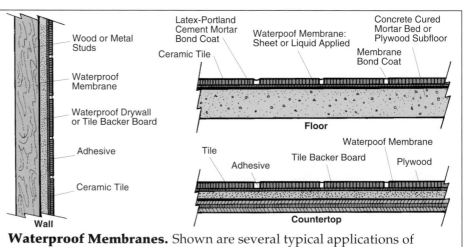

Waterproof Membranes. Shown are several typical applications of waterproof membranes. Seek professional advice concerning your particular tile installation.

floors

Planning the Layout

While many experienced tile-setters simply take measurements of the room, order the correct amount of tile, and compensate for any layout problems during installation, it is usually best for the novice to first plan the layout on paper. A scale drawing will enable you to visualize what the installation will look like before beginning the job. It also will help when it comes to estimating the number of tiles needed, and correcting any layout problems in advance, before working lines have been established on the floor itself. Check to make sure that the floor is reasonably square (all walls meeting at 90-degree angles) and level.

1 Checking Floor for Square. In small rooms, such as a bathroom, the squareness of the floor can be checked with a framing square positioned at each corner of the room. For larger rooms, use the 3-4-5 triangle method. Measure along one wall at floor level to a distance of exactly 3 feet; then along the other wall to a distance of exactly 4 feet. Mark these distances, then take a diagonal measurement between the two. If the distance is exactly 5 feet, the two walls are square to each other. Repeat the process at the other inside corners of the room.

If the floor is less than ⅛ inch out of square in 10 feet, usually it can be compensated for by adjusting the working lines to which the tiles will be laid. If it is more than ⅛ inch out of square, the condition will be visibly noticeable along at least one wall. The cuts will end up tapered. If this is the case, plan the layout so the tapered tiles are positioned along the least noticeable wall in the room.

2 Checking Floor for Level. Use a 2-foot level to check the floor along each of the walls. An out-of-level floor does not present a serious problem unless the tiles will go up a wall. If such is the case, consider

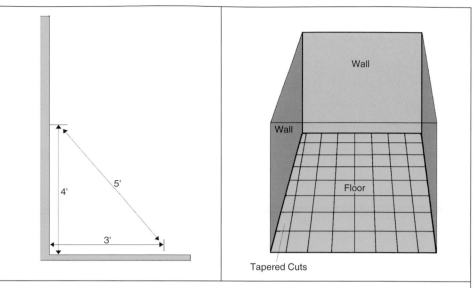

1 Use 3-4-5 triangle method at each corner of the room to determine if walls are square to each other (left). If two adjoining walls are not square, tiles along one of them will be tapered. Plan the layout so the tapered tiles run along the least noticeable wall (right).

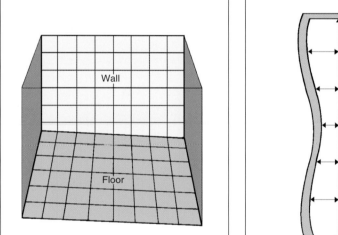

2 If floor is not level, the bottom row of wall tiles will be tapered. You may want to use a different type of wallcovering.

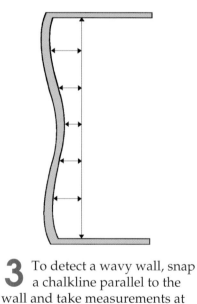

3 To detect a wavy wall, snap a chalkline parallel to the wall and take measurements at intervals along the line.

using a continuous baseboard and a different type of wallcovering.

3 Checking for Wavy Walls. Bear in mind that even if the walls are reasonably square to each other, they may be bowed or wavy, which may also be noticeable when the tile is installed. If this condition is not already apparent from looking at the existing floorcovering, a bowed or wavy condition often can be detected by simply sighting down the wall at floor level. Or, snap a chalkline along the floor, parallel to the wall, and take measurements at various points along the wall. In extreme cases, you may want to remove the existing wall material and shim out the studs to correct the condition, then install a new wallcovering.

4 Making a Scale Drawing.

Measure the overall dimensions of the floor and make a scale drawing of it on graph paper. Be sure to indicate the locations of entryways and any built-in cabinets or other permanent fixtures. Measure the size of the tile itself plus the width of one grout joint. This basic measuring "unit" is used to plan the layout and estimate the amount of tile needed.

Each square on the graph paper represents one square tile and grout joint. If the tile is rectangular, have one square equal the short dimension and two squares for the long dimension. Tiles with irregular shapes, such as a hexagon, are generally sold by the square foot, so it is easy to figure out the amount needed. For a more accurate estimate, lay out a few tiles on the floor to see how many fill in a square space of arbitrary dimensions. Then, on the scale drawing, divide the room into squares of that dimension, count the number of squares in the room, and multiply by the number of tiles in each square. When laying out an octagon-and-square pattern, treat each square on the graph paper as one octagon tile and one square tile.

Using the measuring unit as a guide, make a base drawing of the room dimensions on the graph paper. Then, on a tracing-paper overlay, make a second scale drawing of the tile design to the same dimensions. If you want to experiment with different patterns, now is the time to do it.

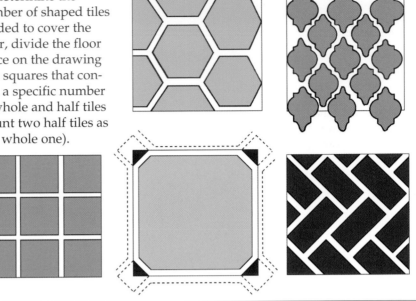

Determining Number of Tiles Needed

To determine the number of shaped tiles needed to cover the floor, divide the floor space on the drawing into squares that contain a specific number of whole and half tiles (count two half tiles as one whole one).

The drawing can be used to determine where cut tiles will be needed. Because few cases exist where tile cuts are unnecessary, plan the layout so that a narrow row of cut tiles in a visually conspicuous place, such as at a doorway, does not result. Any cut pieces should be more than ½ tile wide, and in most cases, cut tiles at opposite sides of the room should be the same width, to provide symmetry. If a full row of tiles are laid along one wall, a narrow row of partial tiles may result along the opposite wall. In some cases, the narrow row may be eliminated by adjusting the width of all the grout joints. Otherwise, adjust the pattern so you end up with wider partial tiles on each opposite wall. Similarly, if the tiles are laid from the exact center of the room out toward each wall, you may end up with narrow cut tiles at both walls. In this case, shift the original centerline ½ tile to the left or right.

Try to center the tiles across large openings, or beneath focal points. If the tiles will extend into an adjacent room, lay out both floors so the grout joints line up at entryways. The drawing can be used as a general guide for establishing the actual working lines on the floor. (See page 35.)

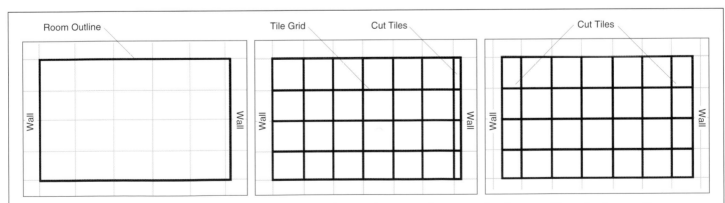

Room Outline · Tile Grid · Cut Tiles · Cut Tiles · Wall

4

If one wall ends up with a narrow row of cut tiles as shown in the example above, adjust the layout line so tiles at opposite ends of room are wider than one half tile. If there are narrow tiles at both ends of the room, "remove" one whole row of tiles and adjust the layout line.

Estimating Amounts

Once the plan is on paper, use it to estimate the amount of tiles, adhesive, and grout that is needed. Tile, no matter what size or shape, is often sold by the square foot. It would be easy enough to simply measure the square footage of the room, make an estimate, then order and additional 10 percent to cover waste due to cut tiles and breakages. This formula works most of the time, provided the installation does not require too many cut tiles, and the tiles are set with grout joints that have been recommended by the tile manufacturer.

To get a more precise measurement, work from the layout drawing by counting the actual number of whole tiles and partial tiles, then add about 5 percent for breakage, miscuts and other mistakes. A layout stick will help when estimating the amount of tiles needed.

To estimate the amount of adhesive needed, simply add up the total number of square feet to be tiled, then check the coverage figures on the label of the adhesive container. The amount of grout needed will depend on the size of the tiles, and the width and depth of the grout joints between them. If provided with this information, an experienced tile dealer can recommend the amount of grout needed. It is better to end up with some adhesive and grout left over at the end of the job, rather than running out in the middle of the job and having to run back to the tile store for more.

Thresholds

Because tiling a floor generally results in a change of floor level, a decision must be made as to how to deal with this change at doorways. Consider how to make the transition where the tile meets different types of floorcoverings in adjacent rooms, whether there is a change in level or not. Thresholds (sometimes called saddles) or transition strips made of metal, wood, or marble are used to bridge gaps between different floors. Depending on job requirements, the thresholds can be installed before or after the tile is laid. The threshold is attached to the underlayment, and the tile is then run up to it. A tile dealer can recommend a suitable threshold for your particular installation.

If the room includes an outside entry door, it may be possible to keep the existing threshold in place and to tile up to it. Otherwise, the threshold can be removed, and tile installed underneath, and the threshold replaced. Then, trim the door bottom to fit. If either of these options creates a visual problem, replace the old threshold with a new one. Plan for thresholds during the layout stage.

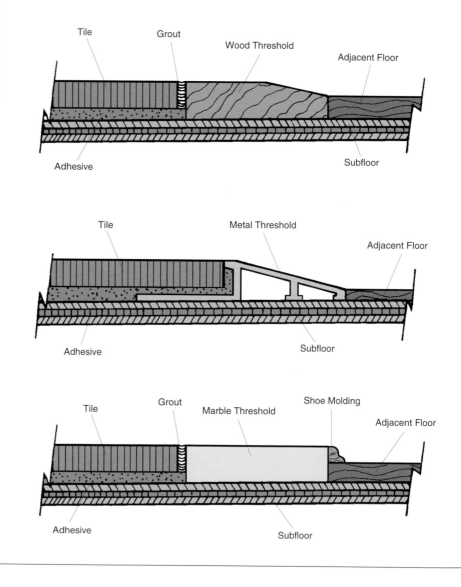

Floor Preparation

Ceramic tile can be installed directly over the existing floorcovering, if the floorcovering, underlayment and subflooring beneath are sound, level, and free from any looseness or buckling. The floor framing must be strong enough to support the additional weight of the tile. Also, the added thickness of the tile will result in a change of floor level, which will have to be dealt with at entryways where the tile meets other floorcoverings (door bottoms may need to be trimmed). A change in floor level may require alterations to base cabinets and plumbing fixtures, such as toilets, when they are reinstalled.

For new floor construction, plan the job to provide suitable framing, subfloor, and underlayment from the start. Any questions concerning whether or not an existing floor can be tiled over should be directed to a building engineer or architect.

Although tile can be laid over an existing floorcovering (if it is sound), it is usually better to remove the floorcovering (if possible), and to install the tile directly to the subfloor beneath. This not only minimizes the change in floor level, it also removes any doubts you may have about the suitability of the floorcovering as an underlayment.

Tiling over Resilient Floors

Ceramic tile can be applied over existing linoleum, vinyl or asphalt flooring (tiles or sheet goods) if it is in good shape (not cracking or peeling) and securely bonded to the floor. Exceptions include cushioned vinyl or multiple layers of resilient flooring, which can compress under the weight of the tile, causing cracks in tiles and grout joints. Do not lay tiles directly over resilient flooring in wet areas, such as bathrooms, because these situations usually require a water-resistant underlayment, often coupled with a waterproofing membrane. On resilient tile floors, remove any loose tiles, scrape off old adhesive from the tile and sub-floor, then readhere tiles with fresh adhesive of the same type. Repair large bubbles or loose areas of sheet flooring by cutting out the loose area with a utility knife, scraping off any dried adhesive, then readhering the piece with the same type of adhesive. Weight down the patch with heavy objects, such as books, until the adhesive dries.

Caution: The clear wear layer on modern vinyl flooring should be roughed up slightly by hand-sanding with 100-grit sandpaper to provide a good adhesive bond. Wear a respirator when working on this project. Some older resilient flooring materials contain asbestos, and should not be sanded.

If the flooring is too damaged to patch easily, either remove it or cover it with an underlayment of ⅜-inch exterior plywood or 5⁄16-inch tile backer board. To remove old tiles or sheet flooring, use a floor scraper (left) or flat tiling spade. Sheet flooring can be cut into sections with a linoleum knife or utility knife for easier removal. Make sure you are wear-ing a respirator. Scrape and pry away the old flooring, being careful not to gouge the underlayment. As the flooring is removed, mist the area with water to keep dust to a minimum (right). Repair surface defects in the underlayment with a floor patching compound. In most cases, an epoxy tile adhesive is recommended for adhering tiles to resilient flooring materials.

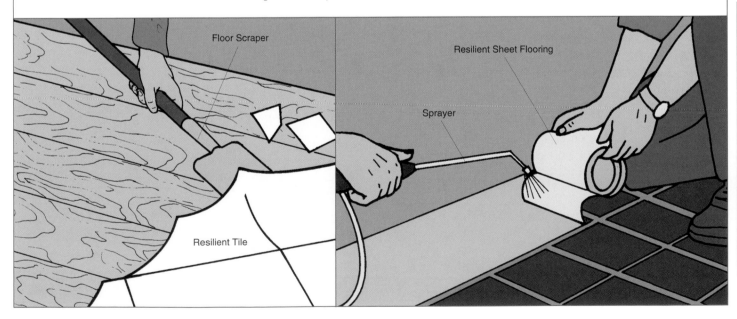

Floor Scraper

Resilient Tile

Resilient Sheet Flooring

Sprayer

3 Floors

New ceramic tile can be laid over old tile if the existing tile is sound and solidly bonded to the floor. Any obvious cracks in the tile or along grout lines usually indicates a weak subfloor or damaged underlayment, which means the tiles will have to be removed and any necessary repairs will have to be made before installing new tiles. If any tiles are loose, pry them up and readhere them. Once this is done, thoroughly clean the old floor with ceramic tile cleaner. To assure a good adhesive bond, rough up the tile surface with a portable power sander equipped with silicon carbide paper. If the grout joints in the existing tile are recessed below the tile surface, more grout can be added to provide a level surface before the adhesive is applied. A tile dealer can recommend the appropriate adhesive for your particular installation. With some adhesives, a thin prime coat is applied using the flat side of a trowel, it is allowed to dry thoroughly, and then a second coat in applied as specified.

Belt Sander to Roughen-Up Tile Surface

Tile

Thinset Adhesive

Plywood

Joist

Tiling over Wood Strip

Ceramic tile can be laid over a hardwood strip or plank floor if it is in good repair and firmly nailed to the subfloor beneath. However, because wood and tile expand and contract at different rates, it is best to remove the flooring or cover it with underlayment. If the floor is sound and you decide to tile over it, nail down any loose boards and replace any damaged ones.

Use a floor sander to remove any surface irregularities (cupped or wavy boards) and to remove the floor finish, providing a smooth, level finish. Clean the floor thoroughly to remove any sawdust left by the sander.

Caution: *Wear a dust mask and hearing protector when sanding.*

Hearing Protector

Dust Mask

Dust Bag

Dust Outlet Pipe

Sander Motor

Drum Cover

Reinforcing Wood-Frame Floors

Before laying tile over any existing floor, check to make sure the subflooring and framing beneath is structurally sound and rigid. If the floor feels spongy or flexible when you walk over it—or if it squeaks over a large area—it will have to be reinforced. If the floor sags, it will have to be leveled.

Even if the floor seems relatively sound, it may need additional reinforcement in the form of larger joists and/or a thicker subflooring. Ceramic tile is heavy, and the added weight may cause the floor to sag or to result in cracked tiles or grout joints. Your local building department can provide subfloor and framing requirements for the type of tile you are using. Typically, 2x10 joists on 16-inch centers provide sufficient support for floor tile.

Spotting Problems. Several factors can contribute to a weak floor. Squeaks can be caused by two boards in the subfloor that have warped and rock when they are stepped on, or subflooring that has separated from the joists. Springy floors are usually caused by inadequate size and spacing joists, girders or posts. Both conditions also can be caused by rotten or termite-infested floor framing and/or subflooring. Inspect the floor from the basement or crawl space while someone walks across it from above. Look for springy boards, movement between joists, and weak bridging. Also check joists, girders and posts for signs of damage. In kitchens and bathrooms, stains on the underside of the subflooring (usually around plumbing fixtures) indicate possible water damage. Bear in mind that the full extent of the damage might not be apparent until the finish flooring is removed. All water-damaged wood should be replaced. The cause of the water damage should be repaired to prevent future problems.

Shimming the Subfloor

Simple wood shims can be used to eliminate movement between loose subfloor boards and joists. Locate the loose boards or plywood subfloor panels (indicated by squeaking sounds) and gently tap shims into the space between the joists and the subfloor to prevent movement. Do not drive the shims too forcefully, or they will cause the gap to widen even more by separating the boards from the joist. Then, nail down the subflooring from the top with 8d nails, angling the nails into the joist.

Cleating the Subfloor

If more than a few boards are loose, or a sagging joist has created a "springy" spot in the subfloor, nail a 1x4 or 1x6 cleat alongside the joist that supports the loose subflooring. Prop it in place with a piece of 2x4 so it will lie snugly against the joist and the subfloor. Then use 8d nails to nail the cleat to the joists. Drive the nails in while the cleat is firmly wedged against the subfloor. After installing the cleat, remove the 2x4 prop.

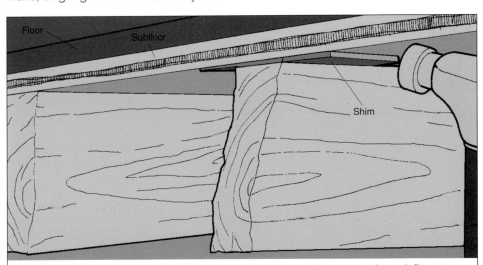

Shimming the Subfloor. If floor joists are not tight against the subfloor in the area that is squeaking, shimming may solve the problem. Wedge shims between the joist and subfloor and tap them into place. Do not pound the shims into place because this will lift the floor and cause additional squeaking.

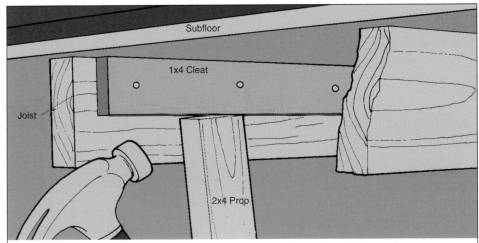

Cleating the Subfloor. Where several boards in the subfloor above a joist are moving, a cleat used to hold them is more effective than shimming the boards individually. A piece of 1x4, wedged against the subfloor and nailed to the joist and the flooring, will keep the subfloor from moving.

3 Floors

Bridging the Joists

If several joists are the cause of a springy or loose subfloor, install steel bridging between them. First, hammer the straight-pronged end into one joist near the top. Then nail the L-shaped flange on the other end into the opposite joist at the bottom, so that the steel bridge creates tension between the two joists. Install the companion bridge in a criss-cross fashion and proceed to other joists. The end result should be a series of joists more firmly braced and less liable to give beneath the weight of the floor.

Bridging the Joists. Squeaking (over a large area) may indicate that the joists beneath the floor are shifting slightly and giving inadequate support to the subfloor. Steel bridging, attached between joists, holds the joists from moving side to side and stabilizes the subfloor.

Replacing a Joist

When replacing a damaged joist, match the height and length of the old joist and be sure the new one is made of straight, structural-grade lumber free of large knots or cracks.

1. Fitting the New Joist. Plane one side of both ends of a new joist to a depth of ¼ inch deep by 18 inches long. Pull all nails from the old joist and remove any blocks holding it to the foundation or to the girder.

2. Placing the First Joist. Fit the planed ends of the new joist on the girder and foundation sill and position it 1½ inches from the old joist on the sill and against the overlapping joist on the beam. The overlapping joist should be firmly sandwiched between the old and new joists. Drive wooden shims under the notches of the new joist to force it up firmly against the subfloor.

3. Breaking Out the Old Joist. Remove the old joist by cutting it with a saber saw near the girder and sill. Use a crowbar to pry the joist loose from the subfloor. Split the ends of the old joist with a hammer and chisel, then pry the pieces out. Pull or cut the nails flush with the subfloor. Then install a second joist cut like the first. Shim it into place.

4. Installing the Second Joist. Use 16d nails to fasten the new joists to the one sandwiched between. Nail a 2x4 wooden spacer between the joists at 3-foot intervals. Toenail the joists at the girder and sill. Install new bridging where needed, then nail the subfloor to the new joists from above.

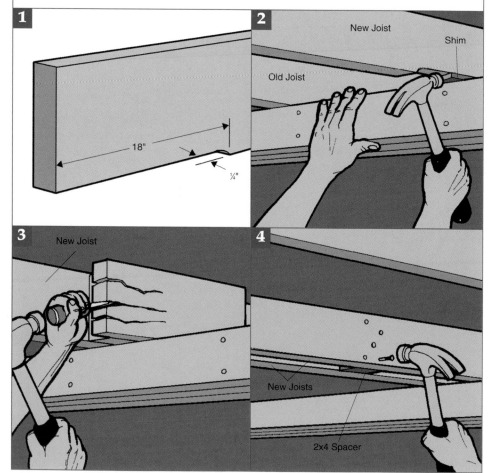

Leveling Wood Floors

Most sags occur on the first floor where the heaviest furniture and appliances are located and where the major traffic occurs. The floor can be jacked up and leveled relatively easily from the basement or crawl space. Repairs to second-story floors are more complex due to cosmetic considerations. For example, in order to fix the second-story floor, the ceiling on the first floor must be removed and replaced. Consult an architect before undertaking any second-story work. For first-floor sags, a telescoping house jack can be permanently installed in the basement to bolster the sag. It functions much like an additional post. For crawl spaces, a smaller, contractor's jack can be used.

Working from the Basement.
To jack up a floor from a basement, first measure the deepest point of a sag by laying an 8-foot straightedge across the sagging area of the floor. Mark this point in the basement by driving a nail through the floor from above. Lock the tubes of a telescoping house jack. Set the jack's bottom plate on a 4x8 pad located beneath the sag point (see below). Have a helper hold a 4x6 beam that will span the joists involved in the sag. Screw the jack so that it presses the beam firmly against the joists. Check the jack for plumb, then nail the jack's S-plates to the pad and beam. Raise the jack only ¹⁄₁₆ inch each day until the floor is level. (Raising it any higher risks structural damage to the house.)

Working from the Crawl Space.
In the crawl space, build a pyramidal framework out of 6x6s until the pad for the contractor's jack lies close enough to the joists to press a beam against the joists involved in the sag. Raise the jack about ¹⁄₁₆ inch each day until the sag is corrected. Make any required repairs.

Replacing a Post

1. Removing the Old Post. If the girder above the post is spliced, cut away the straps over the splice and replace them with two 3-foot pieces of ½-inch plywood. Use 25 to 30 8d nails on each piece. Erect two telescoping jacks 3 feet on either side of the old post and nail the top plates to the girder. Raise the girder ¹⁄₁₆ inch a day until it is completely supported by the jacks and the post is free of any weight. Remove bolts that attach post to girder. With help, tilt the top of the post away from girder so that it can be lifted off the vertical steel dowel.

2. Making a New Footing. On the floor, mark a footing the size required by code. Use a jackhammer to cut through the concrete floor. Remove all of the slab and dig a hole in the subsoil to the required depth. When all dirt is removed, dampen the hole and pour concrete footing while hole is still wet. The concrete should come to a point 4 inches below the floor slab. Release air bubbles by thrusting a shovel into the wet concrete. With a straight piece of lumber, level the surface. Cure the concrete for two weeks by keeping the surface wet and covered with polyethylene.

3. Setting the New Post. Place the new steel column on the footing and adjust the screw so the top of the column reaches snugly against the girder. Use the marks from the old post to center plate. The holes are a guide; drill pilot holes into the girder for the ⅜-inch lag bolts that will attach the plate to it. Tighten the bolts so that the base of the column still moves. Tap with hammer and check for level. Tighten adjusting screw so the post assumes the weight of the girder. Tighten lag bolts. Release the jack ¹⁄₁₆ inch a day until it can be taken down. Fill with concrete.

Preparing the Subfloor

The subfloor should be sound, even, level and free from buckling. It must also be rigid enough to support the tile. Typically, the total thickness of the subfloor and underlayment (if used) should be at least 1⅛ inches thick. If not, build up the subfloor by adding an additional layer of exterior plywood (CDX or better grade) or tile backer board of the appropriate thickness.

Backer board is preferable to plywood because it is less likely to expand and contract at a different rate than the tile, and it provides a better base for various types of thinset adhesives. Backer board is also recommended for wet areas, such as bathroom floors, because it is unaffected by water. Do not use interior-grade plywood or particleboard for subflooring or underlayment—neither material is waterproof, and generally will not provide the rigidity required to support the tile.

If installing a new subfloor directly over the joists, use two layers; one of at least ⅝-inch exterior plywood, the second of ½-inch exterior plywood or backer board, or as specified by local building codes. Be sure to stagger the joints between the top and bottom panels.

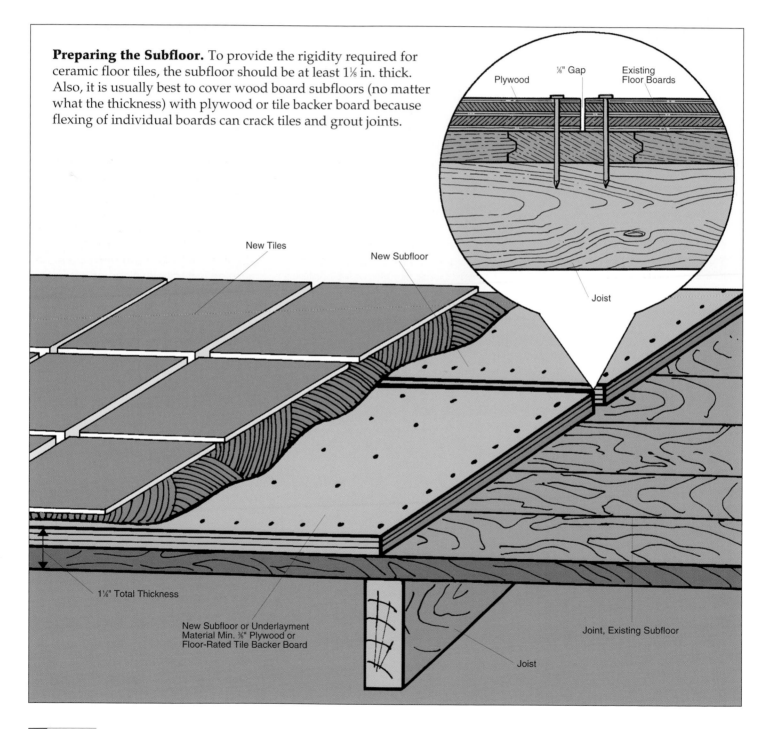

Preparing the Subfloor. To provide the rigidity required for ceramic floor tiles, the subfloor should be at least 1⅛ in. thick. Also, it is usually best to cover wood board subfloors (no matter what the thickness) with plywood or tile backer board because flexing of individual boards can crack tiles and grout joints.

Plywood   ⅛" Gap   Existing Floor Boards

Joist

New Tiles

New Subfloor

1¼" Total Thickness

New Subfloor or Underlayment Material Min. ⅜" Plywood or Floor-Rated Tile Backer Board

Joint, Existing Subfloor

Joist

Installing Underlayment

Because flexing between individual boards can crack tile or grout joints, an underlayment of plywood or backer board should be installed over 1-by or 2-by wood-board subfloors. Such underlayment also can be used to provide a smooth, level surface over an uneven subfloor. Both types of underlayment mentioned should be at least ⅜ inch thick, no matter what the thickness of the subflooring beneath.

If using plywood, attach it to the existing subflooring with construction adhesive and 6d ring-shank nails or 1 inch galvanized all-purpose (drywall-type) screws. If using backer board, consult manufacturer's literature for recommended fasteners and installation methods.

Staggered Joints. With both types, stagger the joints of the new subflooring or underlayment so they do not fall directly over those in the subflooring beneath. When using plywood, a ⅛-inch gap should be left between each sheet and where sheets meet adjoining walls to allow for expansion and contraction. Drive nails around the panel perimeter

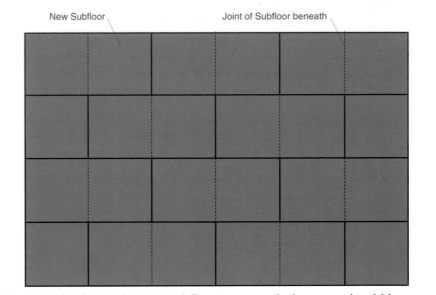

New Subfloor   Joint of Subfloor beneath

Staggered Joints. The new subflooring or underlayment should be staggered so they do not fall directly over those in the subflooring beneath.

about ½ inch in from the edge and 6 inches on center. Then drive them across the face of the panel in rows about 16 inches on center, spacing nails 8 to 12 inches apart. Make sure the nail or screw heads are set below the surface to avoid "stress points" that can crack the tile. Joints between backer board panels are typically filled with tile-setting adhesive and

taped with a special fiberglass mesh tape. Fill joints between plywood panels with floor patching compound, wood putty, or some of the adhesive used to set the tile. After installing the underlayment, sand any rough or splintery surfaces, and make sure the surface is perfectly clean and free of debris before installing the tile.

Underlayment on Board-by-Board Subfloor

Lay the first panel of underlayment across the direction of the boards in the subfloor. If the end of the panel falls directly over a seam in the floor, cut it so that it falls in the middle of a board.

Locate the floor beams in the subfloor by the nail heads and extend their lines onto the underlayment. Drive 8d coated box nails (or staples or screws) every 4 to 6 inches along the floor beams, ⅜ inch from the edges of the underlayment.

Leave about ¹⁄₁₆ inch between sheets of underlayment for minor expansion and contraction.

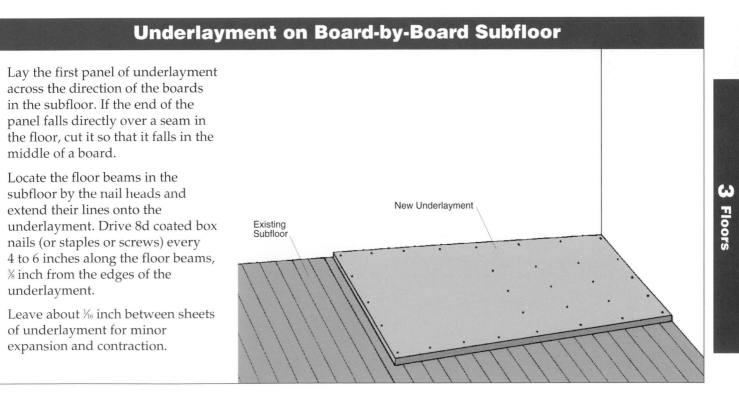

Existing Subfloor

New Underlayment

Repairing Concrete

There are basically two kinds of damaged concrete floors: Those that are merely cracked or pitted, with a structurally sound subfloor, and those that have buckled or heaved due to poor drainage or an unevenly compacted subsoil. The former can be patched; the latter should be repaired and replaced.

A ½-inch layer of new concrete can be poured directly over a flawed cement slab if the subfloor is sound. On a large floor it is easier to pour the new surface in sections, using form boards to divide the room. Align the forms directly over the expansion joints of the old floor. They should be the thickness of the intended surface and may be applied with paneling adhesive which will hold them in place but will let them be removed after the concrete is poured. Cut new control joints over the old ones.

Very small holes in a reasonably sound floor can be patched with an epoxy-based cement. Small holes and cracks should be scraped clean and patched with any of several cement patching compounds. More serious cracks and large holes need more extensive preparation, including breaking up the damaged area and removing the debris. Always use goggles and gloves for such work to protect your eyes and hands. When patching large holes, be sure the wet concrete does not drip onto the good surface and harden there or mar it in some other way.

Filling Large Holes

1 Breaking out the Damage.
To prepare the damaged area, break up the cracked concrete with a sledgehammer or a jackhammer until the pieces are small enough to remove easily. Angle the edges of the hole toward the center with a chisel and hammer. With a strong wire brush, roughen the edges of the hole and remove any loose chips or particles. Enlarge the hole by digging 4 inches deeper than the concrete slab and then tamp the dirt on the floor of the hole with the head of a sledgehammer or the end of a 2x4. Fill the hole with clean ¾-inch gravel up to the bottom of the concrete slab.

2 Getting Ready to Fill. Cut a piece of reinforcing wire mesh to fit inside the hole so that the ends of the wire rest against the sloped edges of the hole in the slab. A few bricks or pieces of debris placed under the wire will keep it at the right level while the concrete is poured. Then add water to premixed concrete until it is workable. Treat the edges of the hole with an epoxy bonding agent and, before it dries, pour the concrete into the hole, pushing it forcefully against the sides of the hole and under the wire mesh. When the hole is filled to the level of the slab, add a few additional shovelfuls of concrete to counter any setting or shrinking. Pull the wire mesh about halfway up through the wet concrete with a rake.

3 Smoothing the Patch. With an assistant, work a 2x4 across the patch, sweeping it back and forth to level the new concrete. Any depressions that occur can be filled with more concrete and troweled level with the 2x4. When the "bleed water" evaporates and the surface looks dull, use a trowel to smooth the final finish. If the patch is too large to reach the center, lay boards across it and kneel on them, moving them back as you go along. The patch should cure for three to seven days. Sprinkle it with water and cover with a sheet of polyethylene to prevent the moisture from evaporating. Check it every day and add more water if the surface becomes dry.

1 Break up damaged concrete back to the solid slab with a sledge or a jackhammer. Clear out the debris, and add fresh gravel.

2 Put reinforcing mesh, cut to fit, up to the edges of the hole. Place a few bricks or pieces of debris to hold it up.

3 Level the patch roughly with a piece of 2x4 and finish with a trowel after the "bleed water" evaporates.

Filling Cracks

1 Clearing the Crack. Some cracks in concrete are not worth the trouble of opening and filling. If a crack is a hairline or slightly larger, patch it with epoxy cement. If a crack is wide enough to get the blade of a chisel into it comfortably, open it up and cut under the sides so the patching material can anchor itself under the beveled edges. Use a cold chisel and a baby sledgehammer. Sweep out debris and dust. Concrete patching material with a latex binder that substitutes for water is usually considered too expensive for large patches, but it is excellent for patching cracks. Follow mixing instructions on the product label.

2 Flushing the Crack. When you are ready to fill the break, flush it out with plenty of water. This cleans the hole and conditions it for the patch so that the old concrete will not soak up water from the new.

3 Filling the Crack. Mix up the material for patching and pack it into the crack with the sharp edge of the trowel, forcing it into all the crevices and undercut edges that you have cleared out. Do not stint on the patching material; pack in as much as you can. When the crack is filled, level and smooth the patch with the flat surface of the trowel.

1 Enlarge a crack with a cold chisel, cutting under the edges to widen it at the bottom so the patch will not pop out.

2 Water clears out small pieces of debris and also seasons the existing concrete to better accept the patch.

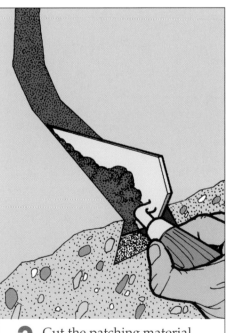

3 Cut the patching material under the beveled edges of the crack with edge of a trowel to fill every crevice.

Preparing Concrete for Tile

To install tile over concrete, the surface must be clean, level, and free of wax, grease, dirt, paint, or other contaminants that may interfere with a good bond.

Caution: Wear safety glasses or goggles.

To clean the surface, use a commercial concrete and driveway cleaner (available at home centers or auto supply stores), followed by a clear water rinse. Chip away minor irregularities, such as concrete splatters, with a wide mason's chisel and masonry hammer.

Caution: Wear goggles, a dust mask and hearing protector while sanding, and vacuum up all dust and debris when finished.

If the concrete floor has been painted or has a slick, troweled finish, rough up the surface to assure a good adhesive bond. Use a rented floor sander and coarse-grit abrasive.

Do not lay tile over a damp concrete floor. If the dampness is surface moisture caused by leaky plumbing or other damp conditions, let the concrete dry out before setting the tile. If moisture is penetrating the slab from beneath, and is a continuing problem, a waterproofing membrane or liquid latex waterproofing compound will have to be installed over the slab. Additionally, a drainage trench may be necessary to direct ground water away from the outside of the slab.

The best time to check a concrete floor for moisture is after a heavy rain. Tape squares of plastic wrap to the floor in various locations. If, after 24 hours, some condensation appears under the pieces of plastic wrap, the floor is too damp to apply tile.

Room Preparation

After you have decided what needs to be done to prepare the floor and subfloor for tile, prepare the room for the work to come.

1 Taking Precautions. First, remove all doors leading to the room and store them so they do not become damaged. After the tile is installed, the doors may temporarily be rehung. Check the clearance at the door bottoms and trim them if necessary. Most often, the installation of tile will raise the level of the floor.

To protect the floors in between the room being worked on and the room that stores the materials, lay down dropcloths and hall-runners. If the job calls for any power sanding or other dust-generating procedures, tape plastic wrap over heating and cooling registers, electrical switches and similar fixtures. Tape temporary sheets of polyethylene over entries to help prevent airborne sawdust from spreading to other rooms of the house.

2 Removing Base Moldings. If the molding consists of a baseboard with an attached shoe, and only the floor will be tiled, then remove just the shoe. If not, remove the entire baseboard.

Starting about 1 foot from a corner, insert a chisel or thin pry bar between the base and wall at nail locations, and gently pry outward. When removing a quarter-round molding or base shoe, use a second chisel to pry between the base shoe and the floor.

Gradually work along the length of the molding until it comes off; inserting wedges to keep base separated from the wall. If the base is to be reinstalled later, remove the nails from the base, patch the nail holes with wood putty, and store the base in a safe place. If the base does not come off easily using this method, then use a hammer and nailset to carefully punch the finish nails completely through the base. Then remove the base, pry out the nails in the wall, and patch the nail holes in the base with wood putty. Rubber topset base (used with resilient flooring) can be removed with a wide-blade putty knife. To ease removal, preheat the molding with a hair dryer or heat gun (at low setting) to soften the base adhesive. In general, there is no need to remove door trims or casings—either make cuts in the bottom end and slip the tiles underneath, or cut the tiles to fit around them.

3 Removing Built-In Cabinets. Base cabinets and vanities usually do not have to be removed. However, if the subfloor underneath the base cabinets and vanity needs to be repaired or replaced, or the tile installation will create a major change in the floor level, therefore affecting appearances if left in place, these objects will have to be removed.

Remove any base or base shoe at the bottom of the cabinet or vanity and run the tile up to it. Then replace the base moldings. If the cabinet has a toe-kick, remove this also. Then run the tile a few inches past it, trim the toe-kick to fit, and reinstall. If the cabinets include a built-in kitchen appliance, such a dishwasher, oven, or trash compactor, remove the appliance and extend the floor tile into the recess. Bear in mind that the tile will raise the height of the appliance, so you may have to raise the countertop slightly or trim the top edge of the appliance opening in the cabinet, if possible.

Running the tile underneath a built-in base cabinet or large vanity, requires a lot of additional work. Bear in mind that a change in floor level also means a change in counter height when the cabinets are reset. In turn clearances between the counter and anything above it (such as a wall-mounted faucet or tiled backsplash) will be affected. If a sink is involved, plumbing connections may need to be modified to allow for the increased height. Before you decide to tile underneath a cabinet, consider all of the alterations that will be required.

1 Seal all electrical outlets, switches, heating registers, air ducts, and doors.

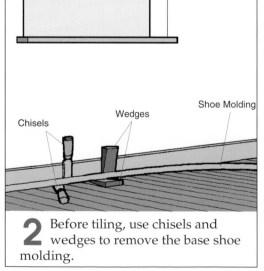

2 Before tiling, use chisels and wedges to remove the base shoe molding.

Chisels   Wedges   Shoe Molding

3 Remove base shoe from bottom of cabinets. Run tile up to it.

Removing a Toilet

The toilet need not be removed when tiling directly over a finish floor (without any changes in subfloor height). As with any base cabinets or a vanity, simply cut the tile to fit around it, then finish off the cutline with silicone caulk. The finished floor will look much nicer if the toilet is removed and the tile extended up to the drain flange.

Taking this extra step may require a few minor alterations. In some cases, the bolts or screws that fasten the toilet to the floor flange may need to be replaced with ones that are long enough to allow for the thickness of the tile, and additional underlayment, if any. However, if the floor flange itself is recessed below the newly tiled surface, the wax ring between the flange and toilet base might not be thick enough to seal properly. If this is the case, the two wax rings usually can be sandwiched together to compensate for the change in height. A better solution is to call in a plumber to reset the floor flange flush to the newly tiled surface.

Before removing the toilet, spread newspapers or a drop cloth around the toilet to soak up excess water that may appear. Also decide where the toilet will be set down after it is removed. Spread out several layers of newspaper in this spot. Before removing anything, pour one cup of chlorine bleach into the bowl and flush to kill germs.

1 **Disconnecting Water Supply and Removing Toilet.** Shut off the water-supply valve to the tank. Remove the tank lid and set it aside. Flush the toilet to empty the water in the tank and bowl. Use a small cup to bail out remaining water in the bowl and tank, then sponge dry.

Disconnect the water supply valve to the tank. Then, remove the porcelain or plastic caps covering the flange bolts and front base screws, if any. Then remove the bolt-nuts and screws. If necessary, use a chisel or

1 Disconnect water supply line, remove nuts on flange bolts, and lift toilet off flange.

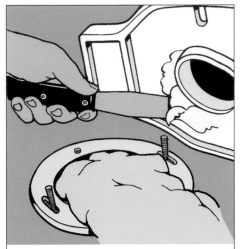

2 Use a putty knife to remove old wax seal from toilet; stop drain hole with paper or rags.

3 Use tile nippers to cut individual tiles to fit around toilet flange.

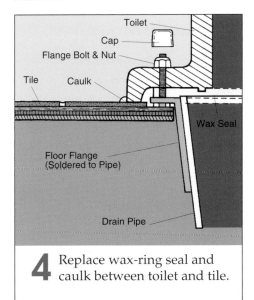

Toilet
Cap
Flange Bolt & Nut
Tile
Caulk
Wax Seal
Floor Flange (Soldered to Pipe)
Drain Pipe

4 Replace wax-ring seal and caulk between toilet and tile.

putty knife to break the caulk seal between the toilet base and floor. Lift the toilet off the flange.

2 **Removing Old Wax Seal.** Carefully set the toilet on its side. With a putty knife or old chisel, clean any wax off the toilet flange. Spray the flange area with a disinfectant, then stuff a rag into the drain hole to prevent sewer gasses from escaping into the work area. Then, duck-walk the toilet out of the bathroom and store in a safe area.

3 **Tiling Around the Flange.** Lay all full tiles as close to the flange as possible. Then, use tile

nippers to cut partial tiles to fit roughly around the flange. The cut edges need not be perfect, since the toilet will be covering them.

4 **Resetting the Toilet.** Resetting the toilet is simply the reverse process of removing it. Before reinstalling the stool, a new wax-ring seal will have to be installed and the flange bolts may have to be replaced with longer ones. Most hardware stores and plumbing supplies carry these items. Do not overtighten the nuts for the flange bolts or the tile may crack.

3 Floors

Establishing Working Lines

Once the pattern has been established, the tile selected, and a suitable surface upon which to lay the tile has been provided, the working lines used to guide the tile installation can be snapped.

Snapping Initial Lines

If the room is relatively square, snap a chalkline along the length of the area down the center of the room. Then, snap a second chalkline across the width of the room so that each chalkline crosses in the approximate center of the room. Check the cross with a framing square to make sure the intersection forms an exact 90-degree angle. These will be your working lines, or layout lines, used to position the tiles.

Starting at the intersection, either dry-lay a row of tiles along each working line, or use a layout stick to deter-mine where cut tiles are needed and what size they will be. Be sure to include the width of grout joints when setting down the tiles.

If a row of partial tiles along one wall is less than ½ tile in width, repo-sition the tiles so that the cut row is ½ tile or wider. If the layout results in a very narrow row of cut tiles, the grout joints can be made a bit wider to eliminate that row. Otherwise, the layout lines will have to be repositioned. (See page 21.) Similarly, if the last tile against the wall is almost the width of a full tile, all the grout joints can be made a bit narrower to fit a full row of tiles in that space. Using this layout method, start laying out the tile from the center of the room, filling in one quadrant at a time.

Lines for Out-of-Square Rooms.

If the room is out-of-square, tiles must be aligned square to at least one wall. To do this, establish a set of square working lines and begin laying out the tiles from one corner of the room. Typically, the lines will be projected from the "most square" corner of the room.

To determine which corner is most square, place a tile tightly against the walls in each corner of the room. Project chalk lines from the outside corner of each tile in both directions, then check the intersections of the chalk lines at each corner for square. Choose the one that is closest to 90 degrees. From this corner, measure out the width of two grout joints and snap a second pair of chalk lines. These will be the working lines. If they are not perfectly square, select the longest wall, or the wall that will be most visible in the room. Then adjust the working line along the adjacent wall until the two working lines form an exact right angle. With the above method, the tiles are laid out from the square corner along the working lines which, if the two walls are square, will result in whole tiles along the two adjacent walls and cut tiles on the walls opposite them.

As with the center-cross layout lines discussed, dry-lay the tiles along the two working lines to determine the size of the cut tiles on the opposite walls. If cut pieces will be less than ½ tile wide and will detract from the installation, adjust the width of the grout joints or reposition the working lines to compensate. Bear in mind that repositioning either of the working lines, will cause partial tiles on the wall next to the line that has been moved.

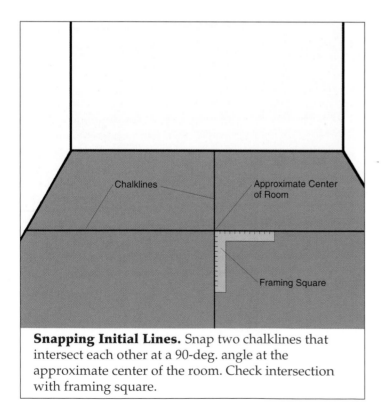

Snapping Initial Lines. Snap two chalklines that intersect each other at a 90-deg. angle at the approximate center of the room. Check intersection with framing square.

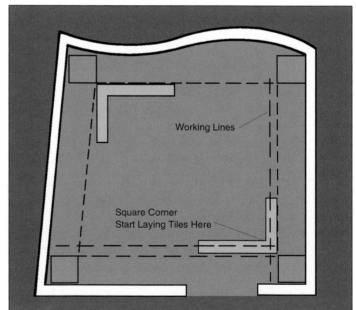

Lines for Out-of-Square Rooms. For wavy or out-of-square walls, place tiles in each corner of room and snap lines between them. Measure in grout joints to establish working lines. Start tiling from square corner.

Lines for L-Shaped Rooms. Divide the room into two squares, and snap layout lines as shown. Adjust the lines so that all intersections are at 90 degrees. Adjust lines as necessary so that cut tiles around the room perimeter will be larger than ½ tile.

Lines for Adjoining Rooms. When extending the tile into an adjoining room, make sure the grout joints line up between the two rooms. If the entrance is wide, try to center the tiles so that any cut tiles at each side are of the same width.

Lines for Large Tiles. Large, irregular-size quarry tiles and pavers generally require additional working lines to ensure that the grout joints align properly and are of approximately the same width. Typically, extra chalk lines are added to form a grid. Each square in the grid can contain four, six, or nine tiles; the lines represent the middle of the grout joints between the tiles. When setting the tile, fill in one block at a time, adjusting the tiles until all of the grout joints are evenly spaced.

Lines for Diagonal Layouts. When laying tiles diagonally, a second set of working lines will be required. From the intersection of the original working lines, measure out an equal distance along any three of the lines, and drive a nail at these points (A, B and C, on the drawing). Hook the

end of a tape measure to one of the nails and hold a pencil against the tape measure at a distance equal to that between the nails and centerpoint. Use the tape measure and pencil as a compass to scribe two sets of arcs on the floor.

Snap two diagonal chalk lines; one between the center intersection and point D on the drawing below, and one between the center intersection and point E. Extend these lines in each direction to the four walls. Erase or cross out the original working lines and lay the tile to the diagonal ones. Use your layout stick or rows of actual tiles to determine the size of cut tiles at the walls. Adjust the working lines, if necessary, to achieve the best pattern of partial tiles at all four walls. When setting the tiles, fill in one quadrant at a time, using the sequence shown below. In a diagonal layout, the cut tiles will always end up against the walls. Ideally, these will be full diagonal half tiles.

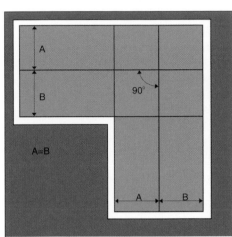

Lines for L-Shaped Rooms.
Working lines for an L-shaped room bisect both "legs" of the L. As with a square room, adjust the lines to avoid narrow cuts along walls, and start laying tiles at the intersection of the two lines, filling in one section at a time.

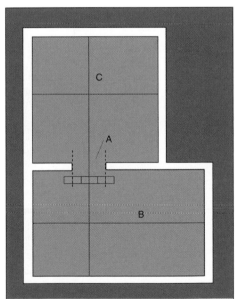

Lines for Adjoining Rooms.
When tiling the floors of adjacent rooms, grout joints should line up. If tiles are large, line A may be adjusted so that they are centered symmetrically across the opening.

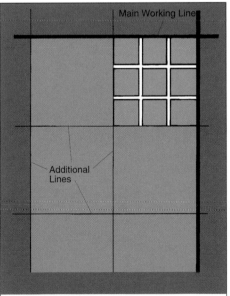

Lines for Large Tiles. Large, irregularly shaped quarry tiles or pavers with wide grout joints are easier to lay out if secondary working lines are provided. Fill in each block with tiles, one at a time.

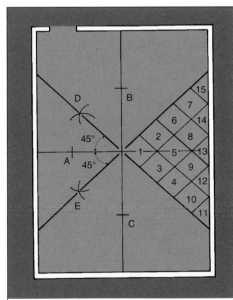

Lines for Diagonal Layouts.
A second set of working lines will be needed for a diagonal layout. (See above text.) Fill in each diagonal quadrant in the numerical sequence shown.

Laying the Tiles

Once the working lines are established, collect all of the tools and materials needed to lay the tile and grout the joints (for a complete description of these procedures, see pages 10–18). Stack the tiles neatly in a convenient location near the work area. Be sure to order extra tiles for mistakes and for cutting trim pieces.

Caution: *When working with an organic adhesive or other volatile or toxic material, provide plenty of ventilation and wear a respirator and safety gloves.*

Before spreading the adhesive, it is a good idea to lay out tiles or sheets of tile in a dry run. If the room is large, lay a single row of tiles along each of the working lines to the wall. Use a layout stick or the chosen spacers to include the width of the grout joints. The dry run is a means of double-checking the accuracy of the layout lines, to make sure all the tiles will be positioned properly and all cut tiles at walls are ½ tile wide or wider. (See page 34.) If the room is small, you might want to dry-lay all the tiles to see how they fit, then make any cuts necessary, so all the cut tiles are ready in advance. If you choose to do this, be sure to key the tiles to their locations by marking corresponding numbers on the back of each tile and on the floor.

1 **Using Battens.** The appearance of the finished job depends on how accurately the first few tiles are set and aligned. To keep the first rows straight, nail 1x2 or 1x3 battens along the working lines at the chosen starting point. (If the floor is concrete, glue down the battens with some of the tile adhesive). Be sure the battens form a perfect right angle.

2 **Spreading Adhesive.** Do not apply more adhesive than can be covered with tile before the adhesive sets up. The area that can be covered depends both on the working time or "open" time of the adhesive, as well as the speed at which tiles are laid. Start by covering a small area (1 square yard), then work up to larger areas. Use the method and notched-trowel size recommended by the tile dealer or manufacturer. Some adhesives are spread at an angle to the tile; others are spread in overlapping arcs. Be careful not to cover the working lines with adhesive—and spread only a little bit of adhesive near the wood batten guides (if they have been installed). For extra-thick tile or tile that has a deep-ridged back pattern, the backside should be "buttered" with adhesive in addition to that on the floor.

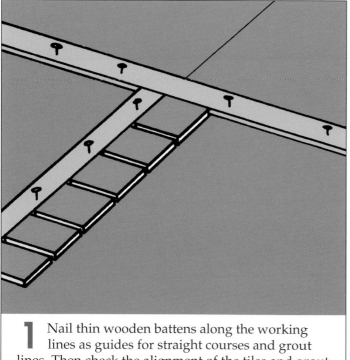

1 Nail thin wooden battens along the working lines as guides for straight courses and grout lines. Then check the alignment of the tiles and grout lines as you work.

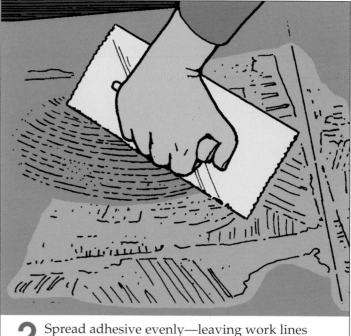

2 Spread adhesive evenly—leaving work lines visible—with a notched trowel that meets the adhesive manufacturer's specifications.

3 Laying Whole Tiles. After spreading the adhesive, press each tile into place, twisting it slightly to bed it firmly into the adhesive. Do not slide the tiles against each other as excess adhesive will build up in the grout joints.

Frequently check for alignment with a straightedge and framing square. Do not panic if they are a bit out of alignment; just wiggle them on the setting bed until they are true. To ensure that the tiles are flat and firmly embedded in the adhesive use a beating block. Slide the block across the tiled surface while tapping it lightly with a hammer or rubber mallet. Check tiles frequently with a straightedge to make sure they are level with each other. If a tile "sinks" below the surface of surrounding tiles, remove it, add more adhesive, then reset it. As you lay tiles closer to the wall corners, space will become more limited. If you must walk over tiles already set, lay a sheet of plywood or particleboard over them to help distribute the weight.

4 Cutting Tiles. When all of the full tiles are down, cut and place all of the partial tiles around the room perimeter. Unless cove or trim tiles will be installed, the cut field tiles butt directly against the wall (with a slight gap between tile and wall for expansion). Install any trim tiles first, then cut pieces of field tile to fit between the trim and the last row of full tiles.

To cut partial field tiles, take two loose tiles (tiles A and B on drawings) and a pencil. Place tile A directly on top of the full-size tile next to the space to be filled. Place tile B on top of tile A; then move tile B up against the wall. Using the edge of tile B as a guide, draw a line on the surface of tile A. The exposed portion of tile A will be used. From the initial mark that was made, measure back a distance equal to two grout joints. Mark a second, parallel line; the cut line. This procedure can be used for cutting L-shaped tiles at outside corners, and for fitting partial tiles between full tiles and cove or trim strips.

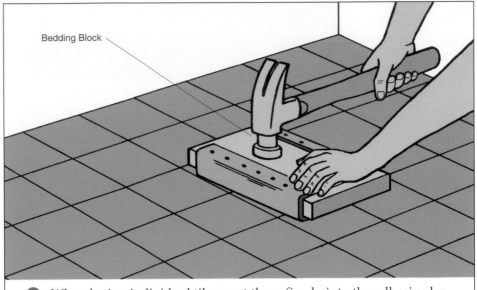

Bedding Block

3 When laying individual tiles, seat them firmly into the adhesive by tapping on a bedding block covered with padding or old carpet.

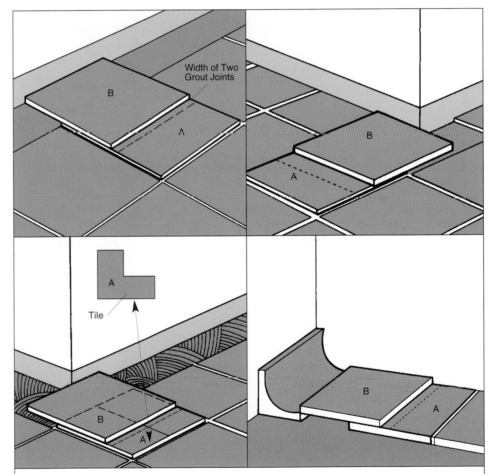

Width of Two Grout Joints

Tile

4 Position full tile (A) over the tile adjacent to the space being fitted. Adjust the tile right or left to align with the space. Place another full tile (B) over tile A in position. Mark and cut tile A (top left). Fitting to the outside corner is done the same, only in two directions (top right, bottom left). If there is a corner finished piece, slide tile B to the edge of the trim; mark tile A. Allow for grout lines; then cut tile A (bottom right).

5 Spread grout across tiles with a rubber float, pressing grout into spaces between tiles (left). Work diagonally across the floor, removing the grout from the surface with a float (middle). After the bulk of the excess grout is removed, clean the tile with a sponge, rinsing it often (right).

5 **Applying the Grout.** Before grouting, allow the adhesive to cure for at least 24 hours, or the time specified by the adhesive manufacturer. Then, clean any debris from the joints and, if necessary, remove any spacers. To prevent the grout from staining the tile surface, unglazed floor tiles should be sealed with a sealant that has been recommended by the tile manufacturer. Make sure the sealer has cured fully before applying the grout. Do not use grout to fill the joint between the last row of floor tiles and the wall. Instead, use a flexible silicone caulk to allow for expansion and contraction between the two.

Mix the grout according to manufacturer's instructions. Use a rubber float or squeegee to spread the grout diagonally across the joints between the tile, packing the grout firmly into every joint. As soon as the grout becomes firm, use a wet sponge to wipe off excess grout from the tile surface.

6 **Tooling.** Shape the grout joints with a striking tool (for instance, a toothbrush handle, spoon, shaped stick). Then, clean off the tiles again and smooth (dress) the joints with a

6 Smooth the grout between tiles with any rounded tool—the handle of a toothbrush works well—leaving a slight depression.

7 Unglazed tile absorbs stains and should be sealed with a sealant specified for that purpose. Apply it with a foam-rubber roller.

damp sponge. Allow a dry haze to form on the tile surface, then polish the tiles with a clean, damp cloth. In most cases, the grout will take several days to a week or more to cure completely; check the manufacturer's recommendations.

7 **Sealing.** If the tile and grout joints require a sealer, apply it according to label directions. (See page 17.) Usually, it takes at least

two weeks for the grout to fully cure before applying a sealer. Make sure the floor is clean and completely dry. Starting in the corner farthest away from the door, apply a thin, even coat of sealer with a foam-rubber paint roller or sponge. Wipe off any excess to prevent discoloration of the tile. After the sealer has dried, apply a tile wax to bring out the beauty of the tile installation.

walls

Tile Layout

While creating a layout for walls is similar to laying out a floor, walls are more likely to have a special design. This not only makes estimating the number of tiles more difficult, but requires a more precise layout. Also, walls typically involve various types of trim tiles, which must also be figured into the layout scheme. (See page 8.)

If both the walls and the floor will be tiled, install the row of cove or other finishing tiles at the floor level first, then do the walls, and finally, the floor. This is so the floor does not get damaged or dirtied with adhesive and grout as you work on the walls above. Preparation for all surfaces (walls, floors, countertops, and the like) should be completed before any tiling begins.

Checking for Square

As with floors, an out-of-square wall will result in a row of tapered cuts along one or both sides of the wall. If one or more adjacent walls are not plumb vertically, a row of tapered cut tiles will be required at the intersection of the two walls. If the adjacent wall is to be tiled, and both walls are out of plumb, the problem will be compounded. Tapered cuts will result on both walls. If a floor or countertop is not level, the bottom row of tiles along the wall will be tapered. The same holds true with the top rows of wall tiles that meet an out-of-level ceiling or soffit.

Use a 2-foot level to check for out-of-plumb or out-of-level conditions. To check the extent of these conditions on adjoining walls, use a plumb bob suspended from the ceiling at each end of the wall, and with a chalkline, snap a vertical line a few inches away from the adjacent wall. Then take measurements. Similarly, to check the extent of an out-of-level floor, use a level and a long, straight board to establish a level line a few inches above the floor. Then take

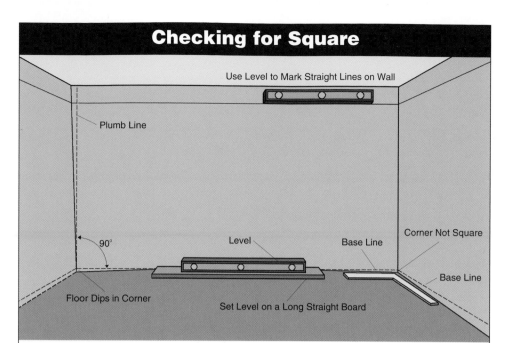

Checking for Square

Use Level to Mark Straight Lines on Wall

Plumb Line

90°

Level

Base Line

Corner Not Square

Base Line

Floor Dips in Corner

Set Level on a Long Straight Board

Out-of-square or out-of-level conditions can be checked. To lay tile, establish a level base line at the bottom of the wall and vertical working lines at wall corners.

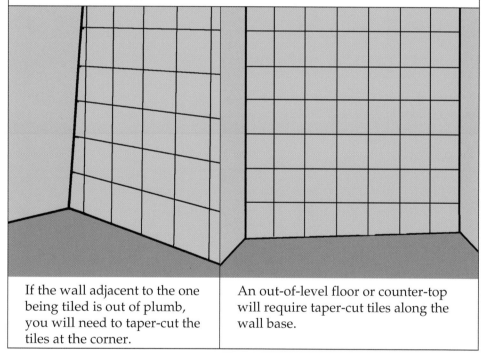

If the wall adjacent to the one being tiled is out of plumb, you will need to taper-cut the tiles at the corner.

An out-of-level floor or counter-top will require taper-cut tiles along the wall base.

measurements between the line and floor at various points.

If a wall is out of plumb no more than ⅛ inch in 8 feet, or the out-of-level floor is no more than ⅛ inch in 10 feet, there is no need to taper-cut the tiles. More serious out-of square conditions will require tapered tiles, unless structural alterations are made to the wall itself. (See page 49.)

Bowed or slightly wavy walls usually do not present a problem unless the floor is to be tiled as well (see page 20–34) or the tile is to be extended to an adjoining wall. However, the surface being tiled should be relatively flat and smooth. (See page 49.)

Making a Scale Drawing

A scale drawing will come in handy for estimating and layout purposes. If the tile pattern will form a design on the wall, it will help you visualize the finished result. First, measure the overall dimensions of the wall or walls to be tiled, then make a scale drawing of them on graph paper; be sure to indicate the locations of doors, windows and any built-in cabinets or other permanent fixtures on the wall. Measure the size of the tile itself plus the width of one grout joint. This dimension will be the basic measuring "unit" used to plan the layout and estimate the amount of tile needed.

Then, on a scaled drawing, divide the wall space into squares using that dimension. Count the number of squares, and multiply by the number of tiles within each square. For figuring rectangular or odd-shaped tiles, see page 21.

Using the tile-grout-joint measurement unit as a guide, make a base drawing of the wall on the graph paper. Then, on a tracing-paper overlay, make a scale drawing of the tile design to the same dimensions. Use as many overlay sheets as required to come up with a pleasing design. Be sure to include the size and location of all trim and border tiles.

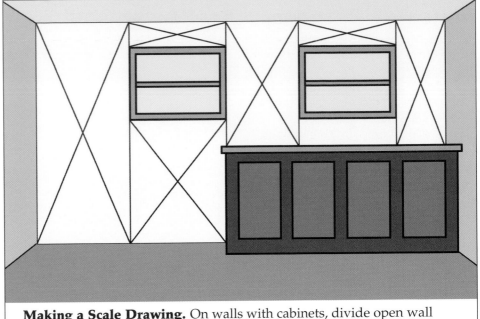

Making a Scale Drawing. On walls with cabinets, divide open wall spaces into squares, then figure the number of tiles required to fill each square. Add these together to get total number of tiles needed. Add 10 percent for cuts and mistakes.

The drawing also can be used to determine in advance where cut tiles will be needed. Plan the layout so a narrow row of cut tiles ends up in a conspicuous place, such as at an outside corner, around a window or door, or above a countertop. Adjust the layout so partial tiles are at least ½ tile wide. Cut tiles at opposite sides of the wall should be of equal width. Also be aware of where cut tiles will be needed around doorways, windows, cabinets, and countertops. For example, cut tiles on either side of a window or door opening should be the same width, so the opening appears "centered" between the grout lines. When planning the vertical layout, it is best to start with a row of full tiles at floor level and above countertops. However, if a course of tile must be cut, make the cut on the first row of field tiles above the base or trim tiles.

Estimating Amounts

Once the plan is on paper, use it to estimate the amount of tiles, adhesive, and grout needed. Tile is usually sold by the square foot. If a drawing of the design is unnecessary and the layout is relatively simple, you need only measure the square footage of the wall space to be tiled. Make an estimate, and then order an additional 5–10 percent to cover breakage.

If the wall has a small window or opening, figure the job as if the wall were solid. If the wall has a large window, several windows, or other obstructions, such as built-in sinks, cabinets, bookcases, or the like, divide the exposed wall space into square or rectangular sections. Figure the square footage of each section, and then add these figures together to get the total square footage; again adding 5–10 percent for breakages.

If the installation includes a design incorporating different color tiles, use the drawing to count the actual number of tiles of each color, adding 5–10 percent to the figure for breakage. If the layout includes cut tiles, count each partial tile as a full tile.

If not working to a scale drawing, a layout stick will help estimate the amount of tiles needed. The stick is also handy for spacing the tiles as they are laid. (See page 10 for instructions on making and using a layout stick.)

Like walls, floors are also difficult to level without making significant alterations to the framing or sub-floor. (See pages 25–29.) However, the effect can be visually minimized (thereby eliminating taper-cut tiles at floor level). Install a continuous wooden base molding (6 inches or wider) along the floor, with the top edge set level, and the bottom edge taper-cut or planed to follow the floor angle or contour. The wider the base molding, the less noticeable the out-of-level condition will be after the tile is installed.

1. From the lowest point on the floor measure up the wall a distance equal to the width of the molding and place a mark. From this mark, strike a level line across the wall to indicate the top edge of the molding.

2. Then measure from the highest point on the floor up to the line on the wall. Subtract this measurement from the width of the base and mark it on one end of the molding. Then mark a cutline along the remaining edge of the board to indicate the amount of taper required. After cutting the taper on the molding, trial fit it to the base of the wall. Use a rasp to remove any "high spots" on the bottom edge of the molding to get a tight fit.

3. When you install the molding, tapered side down, make sure the top edge aligns with the marked line on the wall. A length of ½-inch quarter-round base shoe can be attached to the bottom edge of the molding to cover any minor gaps between the molding and the floor. Set the bottom row of tiles about ⅛ inch above the wood molding and fill the gap with caulk. Tiles on the wall above the base will be level.

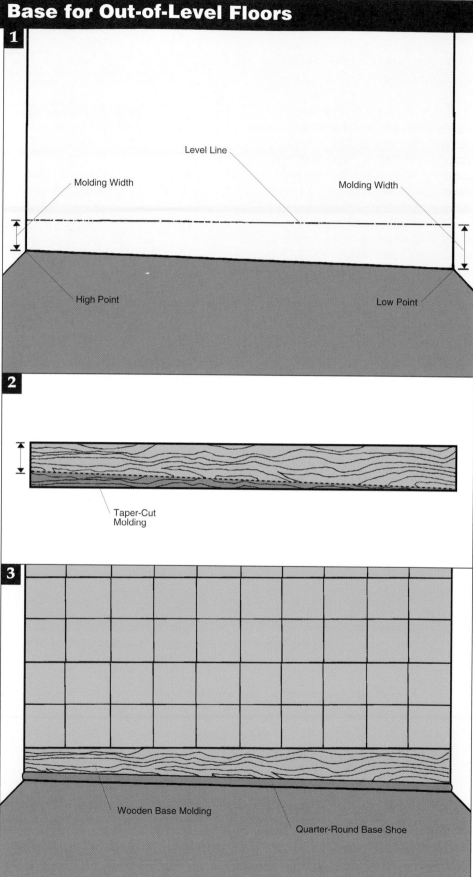

1 Level Line — Molding Width — Molding Width — High Point — Low Point

2 Taper-Cut Molding

3 Wooden Base Molding — Quarter-Round Base Shoe

Room Preparation

The first step in any remodeling job, including tiling, is to make general room preparations to prevent damage to surrounding surfaces and fixtures.

1 Removing Wall Fixtures.
Remove all wall hangings and permanently wall-mounted fixtures, including curtain rods, switch and outlet covers, light fixtures, towel racks, etc. Patch any screw or nail holes left by them. Wall-mounted faucets and supply valves for sinks and toilets usually have a chrome-plated escutcheon ring around the supply pipe to cover the hole where it goes through the wall. Pry the escutcheon away from the wall, use tile nippers to cut the tiles, then slide escutcheon back in place.

2 Protecting the Floor. Lay drop cloths on the floor in the room to be tiled, as well as in other rooms or hallways that will be used during the job. For additional protection from dropped tools or tiles, lay down sheets of thin plywood or particleboard on the floor directly beneath the walls being tiled. Use this method to protect countertops and other surfaces in the immediate work area.

If the job calls for power sanding or other dust-generating procedures, tape plastic wrap over heating registers and electrical outlets. If doors have been removed, tape temporary "curtains" of polyethylene sheeting over the open entries.

3 Removing Trim and Moldings.
The procedure for removing base moldings, door trim, and other wood moldings is the same. Start about a foot from a corner, insert a thin pry bar behind the molding at nail locations, and gently pry outward. Gradually work along the length of the molding until it comes off. If the moldings will be reinstalled, remove the nails, patch the nail holes with wood putty, and store in a safe place. If the moldings will not come off easily, use a hammer and nailset to carefully punch the nails completely through the molding. Remove the molding and pry out the nails in the wall or cabinet, and patch the nail holes with wood putty.

4 Removing Sinks and Toilets. If the sink is recessed into a countertop, it need not be removed unless the countertop is being removed or retiled as well. Freestanding pedestal sinks need not be removed if there is enough clearance between the sink and wall to work comfortably.

Wall-hung sinks can be tiled around or removed. The latter usually makes for a neater installation but, in order to rehang the sink, the mounting bracket may have to be shimmed a distance equal to the thickness of the tile. One way to do this is to use a plywood shim equal in thickness to the tile, cut to the width and length of the bracket. After shutting off the water supply, disconnect trap and supply lines, and lift the sink off the bracket. Remove the bracket, trace its outline on the plywood, and cut out the shim. Nail the shim to the wall at the bracket location, and reattach the bracket with screws that go through the bracket, shim, wallcovering and well into the bracing behind the wall.

The tank can be removed on most toilets, leaving the stool in place. Shut off the supply valve and disconnect the supply line to the tank. Bail out the water in the tank and disconnect the tank from the stool. If the tank is wall mounted, lift it off the mounting bracket, and shim out the bracket.

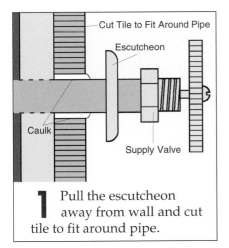

1 Pull the escutcheon away from wall and cut tile to fit around pipe.

Labels: Cut Tile to Fit Around Pipe, Escutcheon, Caulk, Supply Valve

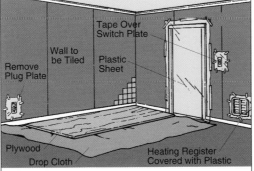

2 To protect the floor, lay down drop cloths and plywood sheets. Cover outlets, heating ducts.

Labels: Tape Over Switch Plate, Wall to be Tiled, Plastic Sheet, Remove Plug Plate, Plywood, Drop Cloth, Heating Register Covered with Plastic

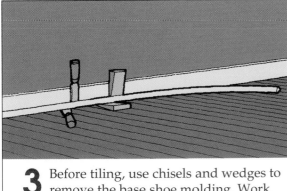

3 Before tiling, use chisels and wedges to remove the base shoe molding. Work carefully if molding will be reinstalled.

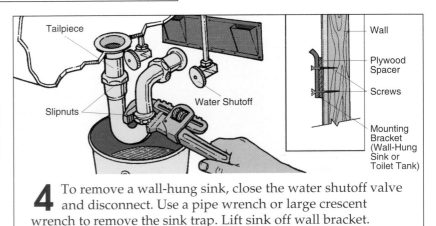

4 To remove a wall-hung sink, close the water shutoff valve and disconnect. Use a pipe wrench or large crescent wrench to remove the sink trap. Lift sink off wall bracket.

Labels: Tailpiece, Slipnuts, Water Shutoff, Wall, Plywood Spacer, Screws, Mounting Bracket (Wall-Hung Sink or Toilet Tank)

Preparing Walls

Most interior walls are surfaced with wallboard or lath and plaster. Both surfaces make a good backing for ceramic tile provided the surface is smooth, flat and solid. Other surfaces suitable for tiling include plywood (½-inch thick minimum), masonry, and existing ceramic tile, provided they are in good shape. Slick tile surfaces should be roughed up with sandpaper to provide a good adhesive bond.

Wood-board paneling and wainscoting generally do not make a good backing for ceramic tile, because the individual boards tend to expand and contract due to changes in temperature and humidity. This movement can cause grout joints to crack. Likewise, thin veneered plywood and composition paneling (hardboard, plastic laminated panels, and "tileboard") are too thin and flexible to support ceramic tile, unless they are firmly adhered to a wallboard or plaster backing. Also, the surfaces of some of these materials may not provide a good bond for some adhesives (plastic laminates or other slick surfaces need to be roughed up with sandpaper to ensure a good adhesive bond). However, wood-board paneling and composition panels are usually easy to remove, and it would be worthwhile to do so, to remove any doubt.

Tiling over wallpaper is trouble, because the weight of the tile eventually will cause the paper to loosen and peel. To remove wallpaper, use a liquid wallpaper remover, or in tough cases, rent a steamer from a tool-rental company. After removing the wallpaper, scrape off any remaining adhesive and rough up the surface with sandpaper.

If you are unsure of the suitability of tiling over an existing wall surface, take the time to build a new one. Fur the wall, and install a new backer board surface.

Surveying the Job

On a frame wall, use a carpenter's level to check for plumb at several places along the wall. Then check it for bulges and depressions by running the edge of a long, straight piece of lumber over the wall. Shining a light along the edge will reveal low areas; a high spot will lift the edge and cause the board to rock. Isolated low spots can be rebuilt with joint compound or plaster. Isolated high spots on a plaster wall can be knocked down with a hammer. If unevenness is widespread, the wall must be furred to prepare it for a new backer board surface. If you are covering a basement wall, decide whether to fur it or frame over it, depending on whether you need space behind the surface.

Lumber

Moisture Protection

It is important that new surfaces on basement walls be as well protected from moisture as possible. If they are wet, you may need foundation repairs; this is not the time to cover them with a new surface such as paneling or wallboard. Damp walls without significant amounts of moisture should be sealed with a waterproofing paint. To protect panels, cover furring with overlapped sheets of 4-mil polyethylene plastic as a moisture barrier. For further protection from moisture damage, seal the back side of paneling. Leave breathing spaces between furring strips on a potentially damp wall. When you install panels, leave a ¼-inch breathing space at the bottom.

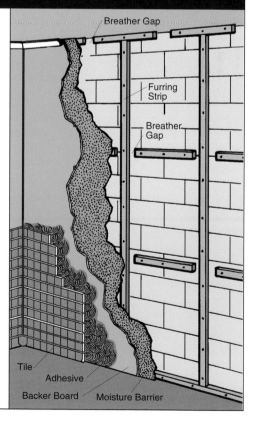

Breather Gap

Furring Strip

Breather Gap

Tile

Adhesive

Backer Board   Moisture Barrier

Preparing Paneling. As mentioned, most wood and composition paneling (such as tileboard or plastic laminate) is too thin to support ceramic tile, unless adhered directly to a firm backing, such as wallboard or concrete block. If you decide that the surface will make a suitable substrate, first clean it thoroughly to remove any wax, grease, oil, or dirt. Then, roughen the surface with 80-grit sandpaper to provide a good adhesive bond. Fill any holes, cracks or dents with wood filler or some of the adhesive used to set the tile.

Preparing Concrete and Masonry Surfaces. New concrete walls should be allowed to cure for at least one month before applying tile over them. If a form-release agent or curing acceleration compound was used when the wall was poured, these may interfere with a good adhesive bond. If water beads up on the surface, rather than being absorbed, one of these chemicals has been used. If such is the case, fur out the wall and install a suitable backing, see pages 44 and 50.

For old concrete or masonry block walls, remove any wax, oil, dirt, or grease from the walls with a mild household detergent or a cleanser recommended by a tile dealer. To insure a good bond, slick masonry walls may need to be sandblasted or bush-hammered with special electric tools. Other general techniques for repairing concrete and masonry walls are much the same as those used for concrete floors. (See pages 30–31.)

A wet basement wall may indicate the need for foundation repairs, which should be done before applying tile over them. Consult a qualified contractor. Damp basement walls without significant amounts of moisture should be sealed with a waterproofing paint. Then, fur them out and apply a waterproofing membrane, followed by tile backer board or water-resistant gypsum board. (See previous page.)

Preparing Ceramic Tile. An existing ceramic tile surface makes a good base for new tile if the tile is fastened securely to the wall. One or two loose tiles usually do not present a problem; simply readhere them with the appropriate adhesive. Many loose tiles may indicate problems with the substrate; remove these and check the backing for water damage. If water damage is apparent inside the wall, leave the area open to dry for a few days to make sure the framing is perfectly dry before reinstalling a water-resistant backing and new tile. If the backing is sound and loose tiles are simply a result of a poor adhesive bond, remove all the loose tiles, scrape off all the old adhesive from the backing, and readhere the tiles with new adhesive. If the existing tile is sound, first use a tile cleaner to clean any wax, grease, or soap scum off the surface. Then, using a carborundum stone or an abrasive disk in an electric grinder, roughen the surface of the old tiles to provide "tooth" for the new adhesive. Finally, use clean water to rinse off the sanding dust.

When tiling over a wainscoted wall or tub or shower surround that does not extend all the way to the ceiling, use one of the methods shown below to deal with the change in wall thickness above the existing tile.

Tiling over a Wainscoted Wall

If you want to tile over existing ceramic-tile wainscot, select a trim profile that will cover the existing trim (A and B). If extending the new tile above the old, build out the wall with wallboard, tile backer board (C) or a mortar bed (D).

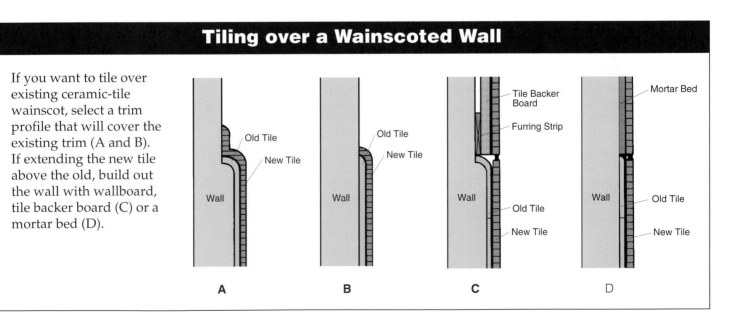

A B C D

Repairing Wallboard & Plaster

Wallboard and plaster walls are subject to a variety of assaults that can damage portions of their surface. Holes, dents, gouges, and large cracks should be repaired before tile is set over them. Damaged areas in drywall can be removed and replaced; loose or damaged plaster must be stripped down to the lath beneath and built up again.

Another problem with wallboard is that as the house settles, seams open and nails pop up. To avoid this problem, drive the loose nails back into the stud, dimpling the wallboard surface slightly to set the nail; for extra holding power, drive nails on either side of the loose one. Cover the dimples with drywall compound or tile adhesive.

The most common problem with wallboard is that as the house settles, seams open and nails pop up and show through the wallcovering. Repairing a popped nail is a simple job: Drive the nail back into the stud, dimpling the surface. To add holding power, drive another wallboard nail into the stud about 2 inches above or below the one that popped. Then plaster over the new dimples. Seams that have opened up should be taped and plastered again. Wallboard repairs require the same tools as wallboard installation and finishing.

Repairing small cracks and holes in a plaster surface is not much different from working with joint compound on wallboard. You will need patching plaster (sold as a powder to be mixed at home) for the base of the new surface and joint compound or vinyl spackling for the finish. The ideal time to make repairs to wall surfaces is when you are about to repaint a room. If you are not refinishing the whole wall under repair, prime the repair and paint or patch it with wallpaper to match the rest of the wall.

Repairing Wallboard with a Wallboard Patch

1 Cutting out the Damage.
Wallboard breaks more easily than a plaster wall. A hard knock, such as from a doorknob flung against it, will cause either a noticeable dent or a hole. To replace a piece of wallboard that is damaged, draw a rectangle around it using a carpenter's square to keep the edges straight and the corners at a 90-degree angle. This will make it easier to get a good fit with the replacement piece. Drill starter holes inside opposite corners, cut the piece with a keyhole saw, and pull it out. If the damaged area is large, cut back to the nearest studs on each side.

2 Adding New Bracing. Cut two pieces of 1x3, each about 6 inches longer than the vertical sides of the hole, as braces for the patch. Insert a brace in the opening and hold it vertically against one edge, centered, so that half the width of the brace is behind the wall and half is showing through the opening. Attach above and below the opening with wallboard screws through the wall into the brace; drive additional screws into the side of the brace in the middle or at 6-inch intervals if the opening is larger than 8 inches. Repeat with the second brace on the other side of the opening. Do not use nails—they will break the wallboard. Cut a wallboard patch the size of the hole, fit it in place and attach with screws through the patch into the braces. If you have to cut back to studs, nail strips of 1x2 flush against their edges to provide a nailing surface for the patch.

3 Taping and Feathering the Patch. Finish the seams around the patch with tape and joint compound. Applying successively wider layers of compound on each side of tape, or "feathering," helps blend the seam into bare wallboard.

1 Drill a starter hole in the corners of the outline and cut out the damaged piece. Leave a neat hole to fill.

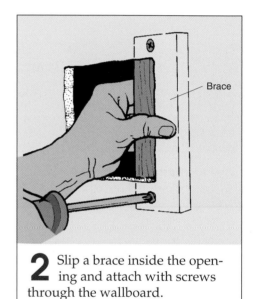

Brace

2 Slip a brace inside the opening and attach with screws through the wallboard.

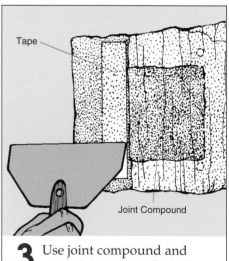

Tape

Joint Compound

3 Use joint compound and paper joint tape to hide the edges of the patch.

Repairing Wallboard with Patching Plaster

1 **Inserting the Screen.** Fix an 18-inch length of string through a piece of ordinary wire screen cut slightly larger than the hole to be repaired. Clear any loose gypsum and wallboard paper from the edge of the hole. Wet the edge on the inside and coat liberally with patching plaster, then put the screen through the hole and pull it flat against the new plaster.

2 **Plastering over the Screen.** Tie the screen to a dowel, pencil or other similar anchor to hold it. Plaster the screen not quite flush with the wall, then tighten the string slightly by twisting the anchor. Allow to dry for a few hours.

3 **Cutting the String.** After the plaster is well set, cut the string at the screen. Moisten the plaster around the edge of the remaining hole and fill with plaster. Apply a second coat over the entire patch to make it almost flush with the wall and let it dry.

4 **Finishing the Patch.** Use joint compound to finish the repair, covering the hole and feathering the edges as in taping wallboard joints. Let dry for a day, then sand smooth.

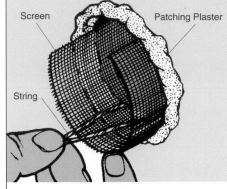

1 Coat the edges of the hole with patching plaster before inserting the screen so it will be fixed to the wall.

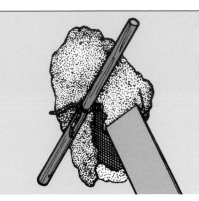

2 Pull the screen flush with the wall, tighten it, and cover with a layer of patching plaster.

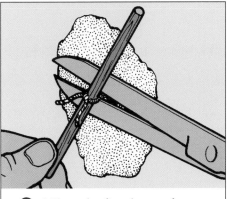

3 When the first layer of plaster is dry, cut away the string and apply a second layer of plaster.

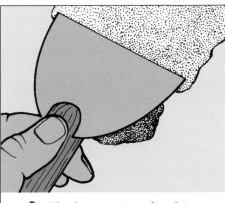

4 The last step is a finishing coat of joint compound. Allow this to dry 24 hours before sanding.

Filling a Crack

1. If the crack is only a hairline, use a can opener to enlarge it slightly. If the crack is wider, follow the instructions for undercutting. (See page 31.) Gouge out a small bit of plaster at either end to seat the patch. Clear out any dust. If the crack is a long one, use this procedure but gouge holes to anchor the plaster every foot or so along the length of the crack.

2. Fill the crack with patching plaster, overlapping the sound wall. Let dry for 24 hours and fill again if the patch subsides. Let dry another 24 hours and sand smooth.

1 Widened Crack

2 Patching Plaster

Repairing a Plaster Wall

1 Clearing Damaged Plaster.
Chip and scrape away all loose plaster around the edge of the hole. Any loose plaster will prevent the patch from anchoring to the wall. Do not worry about enlarging the hole.

2 Undercutting the Edge. Give the patch a sound foundation by undercutting the plaster around the edge of the hole. Do this with a can opener or any implement with a hooked point. Carve under the edge so that the plaster slopes away from the edge toward the lath.

3 Filling the Hole. Moisten the edge of the hole with water. Fill the hole with patching plaster, covering the entire surface of the lath evenly, out to a level just below the level of the surrounding wall. Score the plaster with the corner of a putty knife to make it easier for the top coat to adhere. Let the patch dry.

4 Completing the Patch. When the plaster is dry, apply a coat of joint compound over the patch and feather the edges into the surrounding wall. Allow this coat to dry overnight and sand smooth or apply another coat if the first has subsided below the surface of the wall.

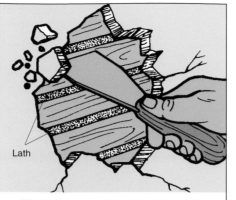

1 Pull damaged plaster away from the hole or impact area. Clear the edges of loose plaster.

Lath

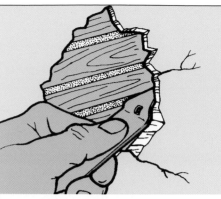

2 Use a sharp implement, preferably one with a hook, to carve under the edge, creating a seat for the patch.

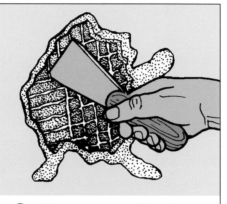

3 When you have filled the hole with patching plaster, groove the surface with the edge of the spreading knife.

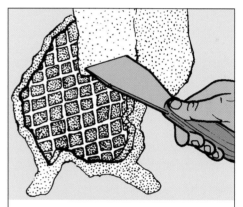

4 Spread joint compound over the patch, filling it flush with the surrounding wall, then feather the edges.

Repairing Plaster at an Outside Corner

If the damage is minor, repair it with joint compound and a putty knife. Where the damage is extensive, tack a straight-edged piece of wood to one side of the corner and use as a guide. Tack far enough above and below the damaged area to avoid causing further damage and gently enough not to fracture good plaster. Fill one side of the damaged area with an undercoat of patching plaster. Use a wooden float to smooth the patch away from the guide toward the good wall; overlap ⅛ inch of the surrounding surface. Move the guide and repeat on the other side. Repair nail holes with joint compound.

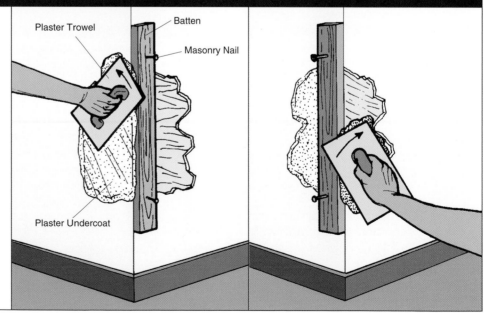

Plaster Trowel

Batten

Masonry Nail

Plaster Undercoat

Preparing Walls for New Surfaces

Before installing a tile surface you will have to prepare the wall to receive it. This task can range from simply removing molding and cleaning the wall, as in the case of frame wallboard walls that are true and without serious surface defects, to building an entire new wall over an old one that cannot be repaired.

To receive a new surface, a wall must provide a flat plane for nailing or gluing surfaces perpendicular to the floor. A plumb wallboard wall in good condition is the ideal surface to tile and is equivalent to a newly built wall. Tile is adhered to the wallboard. Walls with surface defects such as crumbling plaster or unevenness, (for example, concrete or cinder block walls) must be furred out with a lattice of wood to take nails or adhesive. Framing a false wall is called for when you need space for insulation, wiring or pipes. It is useful in basements and garages. A badly deteriorated surface may have to be removed.

The materials you need depends on the wall surface. For furring, use 1x2s and 1x3s which are attached to concrete or cinder blocks with screws into plugs, masonry nails or adhesive, and 8d nails for framing walls. If you must level furring with shims, use wood shingles. False walls are constructed of 2x3s or 2x4s depending on the height of the wall and the weight of the new surface to be attached. Basement walls may require some kind of waterproofing treatment. Drive nails into concrete or masonry block using a baby sledgehammer or drill holes using a carbide-tipped masonry bit chucked on a heavy-duty power drill.

1. Measuring the Distance. Use a chalkline to make a grid where the furring will be nailed to the wall and along the ceiling 2 inches out from the wall at each corner. Hang a plumb bob on the ceiling line at the first stud. Measure the distance from plumb line to each intersection of lines and repeat across the grid to find the highest point on the wall.

2. Attaching First Strip. Attach a horizontal furring strip at the highest point on the grid. When cutting the strip, allow for vertical 1x3s at the corners. Use single pieces, or butt them over studs. Hang the plumb bob above this point and measure from the line to the furring strip. Then hang the plumb bob from the ceiling line at the first stud and shim behind the furring strip until it is the same distance from the plumb line at the highest point. Nail through the shims into the stud. Repeat at each intersection.

3. Attaching Top Strip. Attach a 1x3 furring strip at the top of the wall by shimming at all points to bring it to the same distance from the plumb bob as the strip below.

4. Completing the Furring. Lay a straightedge over the furring strips to find their correct height. Adjust the furring strips so they are flush with the straightedge. Attach vertical pieces in the corner.

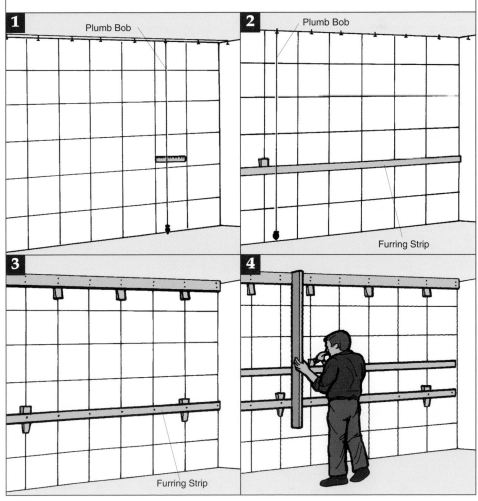

4 Walls

Furring a Wall

Use 8d nails to attach pieces of 1x2 or 1½-inch strips of ½-inch plywood to studs. Over a cinder block or concrete wall use masonry nails or screws into plugs. The grid is usually laid out with vertical pieces 48 inches on center and horizontal pieces 16 inches on center. Leave ½-inch spaces between pieces where they meet, to allow air to circulate behind the panels.

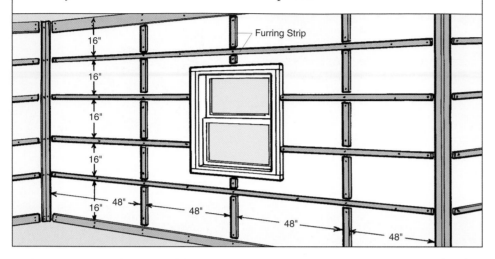

Framing a False Wall

To make room for insulation or wiring under a new surface fastened to a concrete or cinder block wall, erect a frame of 2x3 or 2x4 studs against the masonry. Plan how you will arrange plates at the corners and cut top and bottom plates the length of the wall (or walls). Mark them for stud locations, 16 inches on center. Build a frame on the floor. Then raise it into position. Check for plumb and shim at top and bottom where necessary, then attach at top, bottom, and sides—use 16d nails for wood, masonry nails for concrete. Frame around any electrical outlets.

Furring Windows

1. Removing Molding. If you want to reuse the casing around windows, find the nails at the corners and drive their heads through the adjoining piece with a nail set, then pry the casing away from the wall. If the window has a stool, drive the heads of nails through the horns and pry it out.

2. Adding Furring. Add furring strips around the window on all sides. Because the new surface will deepen the window opening, you will have to add jamb extenders so that molding can be reinstalled on the new surface. The extenders should be the depth of the new surface plus the depth of the furring. Cut a new window stool to fit the depth of the new surface. You can find the dimensions of the new window stool by tracing the old one on new stock. Remember to add the depth of the new wall surface.

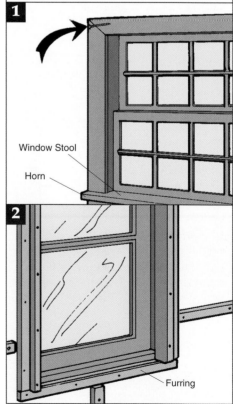

Installing Tile

Installing wall tile follows the same general procedures as installing floor tile, with one major difference: Gravity works against the tile when working on the walls. Always start laying the tiles from the lowest point up, so that the tiles and spacers (if used) support the next course above them. Tiles set over openings, such as windows, will need to be supported by battens tacked to the wall.

Most adhesives used for wall tile are formulated to hold the tiles in place while still wet. These include thinset latex-portland cement and organic mastic adhesives.

Also, wall installations usually require more trim tiles than floor installations do. As previously mentioned, install these before filling in the field tiles.

There are two layout plans for wall tile installation. The most common—and the simplest—has the tiles in each course lie directly above those in the rows below. This is called a jack-on-jack layout. In the second, called running bond, each course is staggered one-half tile over from the one above or below it. This layout requires more cut tile and is more difficult (and more expensive) to install, but the visual effect is pleasing.

Priming the Surface

Once the wall has been prepared for tiling, the surface should be primed to seal out moisture and provide a stronger bond between the adhesive and backing. This bond coat, which in most cases, will be a skim coat of the adhesive being used, or a special primer recommended by the adhesive manufacturer. Apply the bond coat of adhesive with the flat side of a trowel, let it dry, and then sand it smooth. Be sure to pack adhesive around pipes and other wall openings. Primers are applied with a brush or roller, according to label instructions.

Jack-on-Jack

The easiest way to install a jack-on-jack layout is to fill in one row of tiles all the way from the vertical line to the corner, then continue the courses up the wall. Once one half of the wall has been completed, fill in the other. Check the straightness of your tile and grout lines often, using a carpenter's square. If a line is not straight, wiggle the tile back into place before the adhesive has set. The adhesive's setting time will vary according to brand or type; see the manufacturer's note on your particular container.

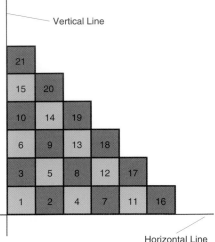

Running Bond

Begin at the vertical working line, with the vertical line running through the center of the first tile that is laid. This is in contrast to jack-on-jack, in which the line runs along the edge of the first tile. Install the horizontal baseline course for the entire wall. You may now complete one row at a time, starting at the vertical working line and filling in over to the corner, staggering the tiles by one half at the beginning of each course.

As an alternative, a stair-step pyramid may be created. However, this pyramid will stair-step up on two sides, instead of one, and will cover the entire wall in one continuous process. Begin row 1 on the horizontal working line. Take three tiles. Lay tile 1 so that the vertical working line runs through the center of the tile. Set tile 2 and 3 on either side of tile 1. To build row 2, take two tiles and place one on either side of the vertical working line. The grout lines between tiles 1 and 2 and between tiles 1 and 3 will fall in the centers of tiles 4 and 5.

Cap the pyramid with a single tile—tile 6—which is cut in half by the vertical working line.

Once the basic pyramid shape is established, add a set of tiles to each side of each course until the pyramid shape is completed again. Always begin laying the tile at the horizontal base line and progressively work up the side and over to the vertical line. This pattern will lend support to the growing weight of the tiles.

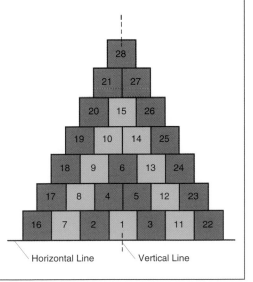

Laying the Tile

1 Locating a Vertical Guideline.
Tiling from the middle of a wall is the easiest method. Your first measurement should be to determine the center of the wall. Lay out a run of tiles, including the additional spacing for grout for tiles with straight edges, but no additional space for tiles with lugs on the edges that set the spacing when butted. Mark the widths directly on the wall. Check whether the last tile on either side of the midpoint is more or less than half a tile wide. If it is less, mark half the width of a tile to the right or left of the midpoint and use this as the position of the vertical guideline.

2 Marking Vertical Guideline.
Use a carpenter's level to mark the vertical guideline at the proper point on the wall.

3 Establishing a Horizontal Guideline. Check whether the floor or tub is level. If it is less than ⅛ inch off from one end to the other, mark the horizontal guideline from the highest point. If it is more than ⅛ inch off, mark the horizontal from the low end. If you are meeting a floor or counter with trim tile, put a piece of trim in position and a field tile on top, held at the proper grout spacing or butted on lugs, and then put a level on the lugs or equal to the grout space above. Mark along the bottom of the level and extend the line to the length of the wall. If you are meeting a tub with field tile, measure from the top of a single piece of tile set on the lowest point. If you need to fit tiles against a ceiling, measure down from the top and use the method above to establish the height to which the first row of tiles must be trimmed. Trim a few tiles to that height, and use one to establish the horizontal above the tub rim.

4 Marking for Accessories. If you are mounting the kind of soap dish, towel bar, or toothbrush holder that sits flush to the wall, find the position where the piece is to be located and mark off the dimension of the part that will sit against the wall. Most pieces have flanges that fit over surrounding tile.

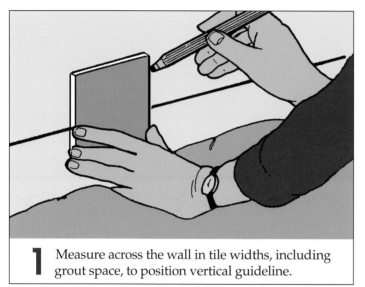

1 Measure across the wall in tile widths, including grout space, to position vertical guideline.

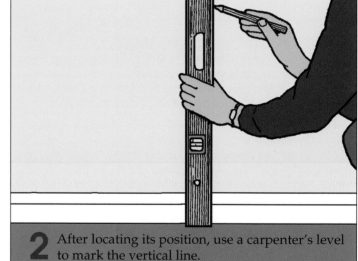

2 After locating its position, use a carpenter's level to mark the vertical line.

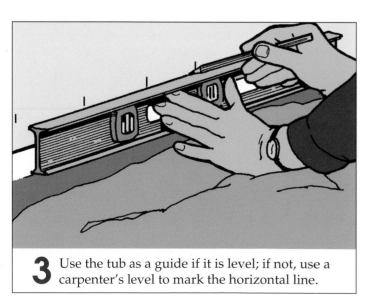

3 Use the tub as a guide if it is level; if not, use a carpenter's level to mark the horizontal line.

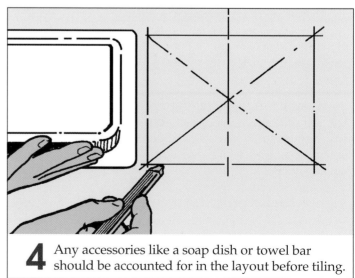

4 Any accessories like a soap dish or towel bar should be accounted for in the layout before tiling.

5 **Applying Adhesive.** Tile can be bonded to the wall with a mix-it-yourself cement-based adhesive or, with greater ease, a premixed mastic adhesive. The basic method of applying a mastic adhesive is to scrape it across a wall off the long edge of a notched trowel. The depths of the bottoms of the valleys at or near the wall surface should be consistent. Start at the guidelines and work your way out, leaving the lines visible.

6 **Finishing Adhesive.** If you are working on a small wall, cover the entire surface with adhesive; if you are tiling a large surface, work in smaller areas. Cover the surface entirely and evenly. The adhesive dries slowly, allowing time to make adjustments. Do not cover such a large area that the adhesive loses its tackiness before you get to it.

7 **Laying First Tiles.** Line up the first tile along the vertical guideline and tip it into position. Give the tile a slight twist to spread the adhesive beneath it more evenly. Settle the tile one half grout space away from the horizontal and vertical lines if it has no lugs; with the lugs on the lines if it does. Set a second tile on the other side of the vertical line in the same manner. If the tile has lugs, butt them. If there are no lugs, use an object of uniform thickness such as a piece of cardboard, a thin wood strip, or a nail. The only rule is that the spacer must be the thickness of the gap you want. Tiles without lugs should be supported with nails under each one. Tiles with lugs require nails only under the bottom row to keep them in position.

8 **Completing the Wall.** Use either the pyramid or jack-on-jack method to position subsequent tiles. (See page 51.) If the tiles are laid carefully along the guidel-ines, their straight edges will serve as in-place guides for the next tiles, and they in turn for subsequent ones.

5 You will need a trowel with V-shaped grooves to leave ridges of adhesive between valleys close to the wall surface. Work out from the guidelines, leaving them visible.

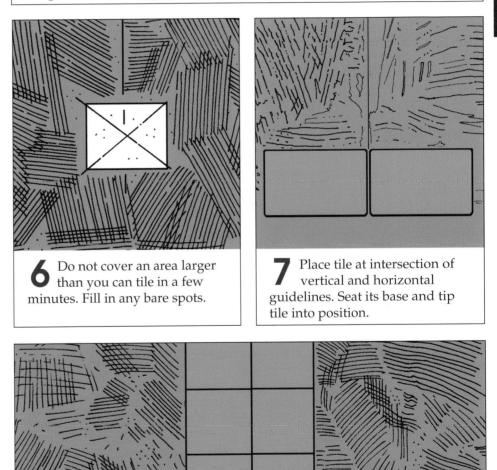

6 Do not cover an area larger than you can tile in a few minutes. Fill in any bare spots.

7 Place tile at intersection of vertical and horizontal guidelines. Seat its base and tip tile into position.

8 Using the first tile and the guidelines for reference, seat the second tile and continue in whatever pattern you choose. Constantly check positions of tiles to be sure they are aligned.

4 Walls

Walls **53**

Straight Cuts

1. Use a small cutter to make straight cuts. The cutter holds the tile in place while you score the surface with a wheel at the end of a handle mounted on a fixed track. Run the cutting wheel back and forth, applying some pressure to cut the surface, then tip the handle back to break the tile along the score line. Always cut tiles with ridges on the back in the direction the ridges run.

2. The cut is likely to have some rough edges which should be squared off with a small piece of metal plaster lath.

Odd Shape Cuts

1. To fit tile around a shower head or pipe, you must cut it bit by bit with tile nippers. This work requires a strong wrist and a lot of patience.

2. Most pipe areas and holes you must cut around will later be covered by an escutcheon concealing the ragged edges of the cut. To fit around pipes, cut the tile into the two sections and nip out a semicircle on both meeting edges. (See page 70.) If you need a very precise circular cut you can drill it with a carbide-tipped hole saw, from the back of the tile.

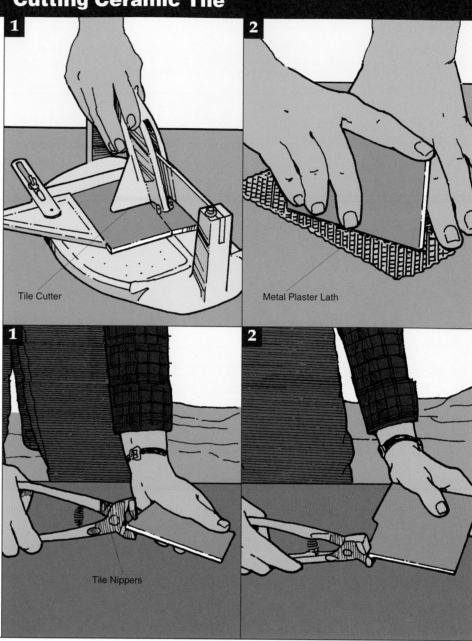

Tile Cutter

Metal Plaster Lath

Tile Nippers

Mounting a Soap Dish

A soap dish or other ceramic accessory should be the last piece installed. The surface must be free of tile adhesive. Soap dishes may be subject to unusual stress. Use epoxy putties or special mastic-like adhesives designed to do the job. The adhesive is applied to the soap dish, then the dish is stuck onto the wall. Drying may take several days.

chapter 5

countertops

Selecting Tile

Glazed ceramic tile makes an excellent countertop material because it resists heat, moisture and stains from food and household chemicals. Thinner ¼-inch glazed wall tiles can be used for countertops in light-duty areas, such a bathroom vanity, but they are usually too thin to withstand hard knocks and hot pans. Tiles made specially for countertops are between ⅜ inch to ½ inch thick (to resist impact), with a durable glaze to resist abrasion and moisture penetration. They also come with the appropriate trim strips for finishing off the front edge. Tiles with a matte finish are generally preferable to those with highly glazed surfaces. The surface texture should be relatively smooth to facilitate cleaning, but should not be slick.

Tiling over Existing Materials

Tile can be laid over an existing ceramic tile or plastic laminate countertop, provided the tile or laminate is firmly bonded to the substrate, and in good condition. Readhere any loose tiles to the counter with the same adhesive that is used to set the new ones. Loose or bubbled sections of plastic laminate can be readhered by carefully heating the loose section with a heat gun or iron to soften the adhesive beneath. Then roll the laminate with a rubber J-roller or tap it with hammer and beating block. Before applying new tile over either material, roughen the surface with silicon carbide sandpaper or a carborundum stone.

In all cases, tiling over an existing countertop will mean a change in counter height and thickness. This may create visual problems at edges (special trim tiles must be used) and it may interfere with the reinstallation of sinks or other countertop appliances. Usually, it is best to remove the old countertop altogether, and to install a rough plywood countertop.

Planning the Job

In most cases, it will not be necessary to make a scale drawing of the tile layout as is often done with walls and floors. Usually, it is possible simply to dry-lay the tiles on the top, and arrange them for the least number of cuts. Before building the rough countertop for the tiles, decide in advance how the edges will be finished. After this is decided you will be able to determine the overhang.

Edge Treatments & Overhangs

First, determine the type of overhang and edge trim to be used. The size of the rough countertop will be determined by the type of edge treatment chosen. Make sure the edge treatment provides enough clearance for opening the top drawers in the cabinets (avoiding finger-pinching situations) and for the installation of under-counter appliances, such as a dishwasher. If clearance problems result, choose a thinner trim treatment or else build up the countertop thickness to accommodate the chosen trim. (See page 57.)

Counters with large over-hangs, such as pass-through counters, serving counters or bars, will require some type of decorative bracing to support the overhang. If the overhang is 6 inches or less, support the top with 1x2 and 1x4 cleats.

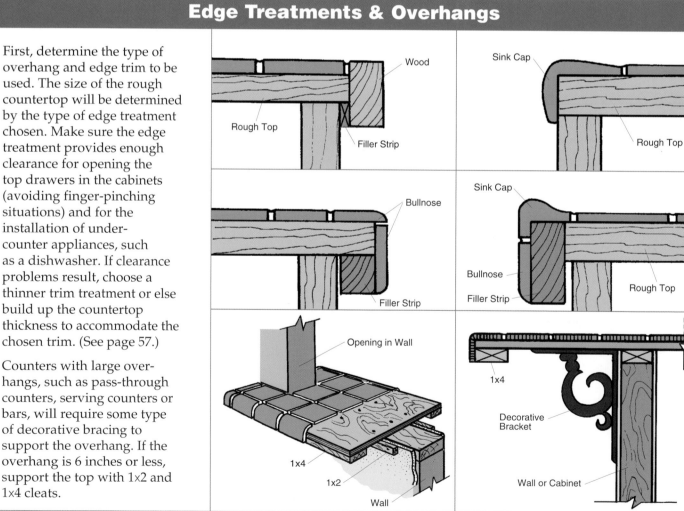

Rough Countertop

There are two types of underlayment to choose from for a rough countertop: plywood or a combination of plywood and tile backer board. The latter is preferable in wet locations, such as around sinks. In both cases, use ¾-inch exterior plywood (minimum B-D). Do not use interior plywood or particleboard.

Because tile is heavy and inflexible, the plywood top must be rigid. Depending on the cabinet layout, additional bracing beneath the top may or may not be required.

1 Installing Bracing. Cabinets or counter base framing should include crossbraces spaced 36 inches apart (or less) for countertops up to 24 inches wide, and 18 to 24 inches apart for wider tops. Crossbraces can be 1x2s on edge or 2x4s laid flat. If the top will be made up of two or more pieces, install additional braces to support the pieces where they join.

2 Adding Trim Strips. If a thicker rough top is needed (to accommodate wide trim tiles, for instance), a second layer of plywood need not be installed over the first. Instead, cut and attach 3- to 4-inch-wide plywood trim strips to the underside of the top, both around the perimeter and across the top where it will be attached to crossbraces on the cabinet or counter base. If the top has been made from more than one piece, reinforce joints from underneath with plywood strips.

3 Cutting and Fitting Top. Measure, cut, and fit the plywood top to provide the appropriate overhang on all open edges. If the top will butt against a wavy wall, cut it to the finish width plus about ⅛ inch more than the maximum depth of the wall irregularities. Then, use a compass to scribe the top pieces, and cut to fit. After cutting the top, add trim strips. (See Step 2.) Depending on the backsplash to be used, a plywood strip may have to be added.

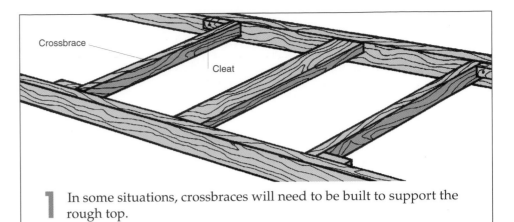

1 In some situations, crossbraces will need to be built to support the rough top.

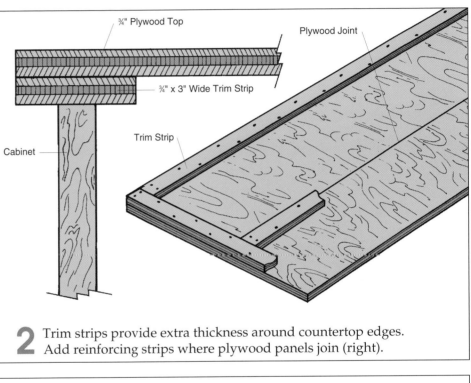

2 Trim strips provide extra thickness around countertop edges. Add reinforcing strips where plywood panels join (right).

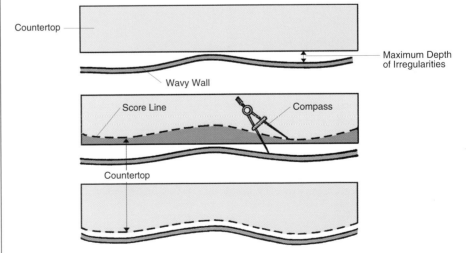

3 To fit the rough top against a wavy wall cut the top to finish width plus about ⅛ in. more than the maximum depth of the wall irregularities (top). Use a compass to scribe top (middle). Then cut to fit (bottom).

5 Countertops

4 **Installing the Top.** Place the rough countertop on the cabinets or counter base and check for level in both directions. The counter should not be more than 1/8 inch out of level in 10 feet. Add shims, if necessary, to level the top when it is installed. Working from underneath, drill pilot holes through the corner braces in the cabinets, or into the braces installed in Step 1. Place the plywood top on the cabinets or base, and screw the top to the base, through the braces, from underneath. Double-check the rough top to make sure it is level. If it is not, back out the screws and add more shims where needed.

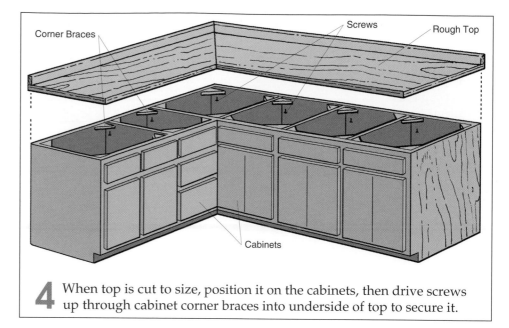

4 When top is cut to size, position it on the cabinets, then drive screws up through cabinet corner braces into underside of top to secure it.

Backer Board Countertop

First install a ¾-inch plywood top as described above. If the countertop will be subjected to water, staple 4-mil polyethylene film or 15-pound building felt over the entire top, or use a trowel-applied waterproof membrane. Then, cut ½-inch backer board pieces to size, using a circular saw equipped with a carborundum (masonry) blade. Nail or screw the pieces to the top, using 1¼-inch galvanized roofing nails or galvanized drywall screws. Space nails or screws 6–8 inches apart along edges and across the counter surface. Where backer board sheets abut, allow a ³⁄₁₆-inch gap to be filled in with mortar. Joints between backer board sheets and all exposed edges should be taped with fiberglass-mesh tape and adhesive per manufacturer's instructions. When tiling over backer board, use an appropriate latex-cement mortar recommended by the tile manufacturer.

Fiberglass Mesh Reinforcing Tape

Tile Backer Board

Drywall Screws

4-Mil. Plastic Film

Adhesive

Adhesive

¾" Plywood Top

Sink Cutouts

If the countertop will include a sink or lavatory, decide whether to install it before or after the tile is laid. This will, in part, determine the size of the cutout. Depending upon the type of sink to be installed, there may be no choice.

Rim Mounts. If the rim is to be tiled over with bullnose tiles, cut a rabbet into the rough top around the sink

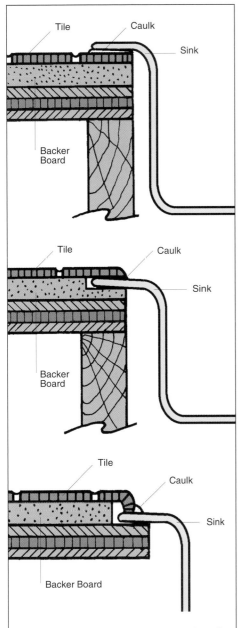

Rim Mounts. Top-mounted sink (top) is least desirable. Recessed sinks (middle, bottom) look better and are easier to keep clean.

opening so the rim sits flush with the plywood surface. A deeper rabbet will enable you to use quarter-round trim, which is also used for recessing sinks in tile and backer board countertops. No matter which method chosen, the sink cutout will have to be made in the plywood top before laying the tile. Also, it is often easier to loose-lay the rough top on the cabinets or base, measure and mark the cutout, and then remove the top for cutting.

Typically, the sink rim should be set back a minimum of 2 inches from the front edge of the counter, and cen-tered between the front and back, if possible. Also make sure there are no braces or other obstructions underneath the countertop that interfere with the sink basin. If there is a problem in centering the cutout, measure to find its center underneath the coun-tertop, then drive a nail up through the top and take measurements from the nail on the topside.

Making the Cutout

1 Center the Sink. Most new sinks come with templates for the cutout. If no template is available, position the sink upside-down on the countertop.

2 Trace the Outline. Trace the outline of the sink onto the countertop. Then, offset the cut lines by the width of the sink rim.

3 Make the Cutout. For square cutouts, drill a hole at each corner that matches the radius of the sink corners, then make straight cuts with a handsaw or portable circular saw. Use a jigsaw for round cutouts. Install the sink according to manufacturer's instructions. Use silicone caulk to seal joints between the sink and countertop, and again between the sink and tile.

1 Center the sink upside-down on the countertop in the desired location.

2 Trace outline of sink on countertop, then subtract width of sink rim.

3 Make cutout by drilling holes in each corner, then making cutout with jigsaw.

Planning the Layout

1 **Test-Fitting Tiles.** After the countertop has been prepared for tiling, loose-lay all the tiles (including trim tiles, if any) on the countertop to determine the best layout. When using square-edged tiles without spacer lugs, fit plastic tile spacers in between the tiles to allow for grout joints. Try to lay out the tiles for the least number of cuts. Work from front to back so that any cut tiles will fall at the back.

2 **Laying out Trim Tiles.** Be sure to take into account the width of trim tiles when laying the whole tiles. If there will be a wood edging, butt the whole tiles up to the front edge of the surface. If the tiles have spacer lugs, there will be a grout joint between the tile and wood molding; if not, the tiled edge will be flush against it.

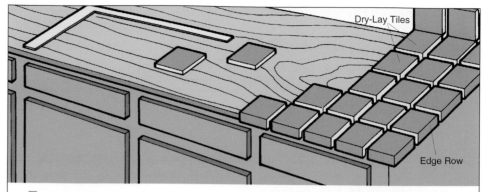

1 Test-fit tiles to determine where any cut tiles are needed. Do not forget to include grout joints.

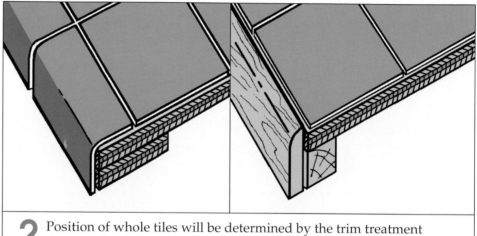

2 Position of whole tiles will be determined by the trim treatment chosen: tiles (left) or wood edging (right).

Countertops with Sinks

Set Parallel to the Wall. Rather than working with the centerline of the countertop, in this case you will work from the center of the sink toward the ends of the countertop. Test-fit the tile, and work for an arrangement that will require the fewest cut tiles. Of course, there is no way to avoid cutting tiles in order to allow for the sink opening.

Set in the Corner. An L-shaped countertop with a corner sink must be handled differently than those set parallel to the wall. Because there is no way to avoid very odd cuts of tile around the sink, the best method is to work from the ends of each leg of the countertop toward the sink opening.

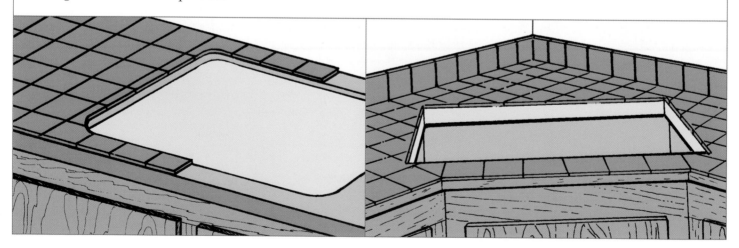

3 Rectangular Layout. When tiling a rectangular countertop, find and mark the center of the front edge of the countertop. (If the countertop includes a sink, use the centerpoint of the sink as the starting point). Then, match the center of a tile to this mark and lay a row of loose tiles on each side along the front edge. If the countertop is open at both ends, adjust the tiles so that any cut tiles at each end are equal in width. If the cut tiles are less than one half tile wide, shift the row of tiles by one half tile width to avoid this undesirable situation.

If the counter is open at only one end, lay out the tiles with fill tiles along the open end and cut tiles along the wall at the opposite end. If the counter is freestanding, plan the layout so the border tiles are equal all the way around.

4 L-Shaped Layout. For an L-shaped countertop, position a tile at the inside corner of the L, and pencil around the edges to mark where the tiling is going to start. This starting point cannot be adjusted, so tiles may have to be cut to fit the exposed edges. Countertops that are L-shaped and have corner sinks usually involve odd cuts of tile to fit the sink edge. (See page 60.)

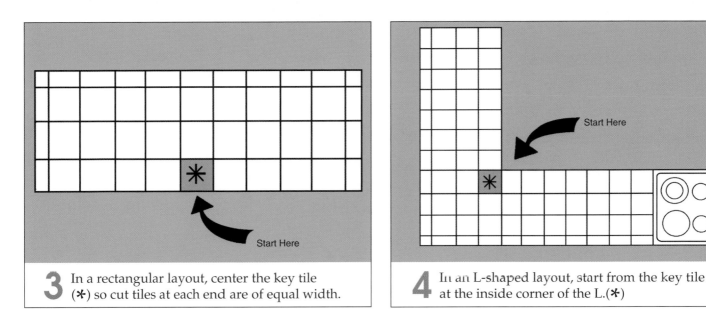

3 In a rectangular layout, center the key tile (✳) so cut tiles at each end are of equal width.

4 In an L-shaped layout, start from the key tile at the inside corner of the L.(✳)

Backsplashes

If the counter will include a backsplash, represent it on the layout. The simplest method is to adhere one or more courses of tile directly to the wall behind the countertop (left and center). The top course can be finished with bullnose tiles or quarter-round trim tiles, or the backsplash can be extended all the way up to the bottom edge of an upper cabinet. If cut tiles are used for the last row on the countertop, butt these tiles against the wall, then place the backsplash tiles on top to hide the cut edges. If full tiles are used for the last row, fit the backsplash tiles behind them, if possible. The backsplash also can be built by attaching a ¾-inch plywood strip to the back edge of the rough countertop before it is installed (right). In all cases, position backsplash tiles to align with countertop tiles. In all cases, use full tiles for the first course on the backsplash.

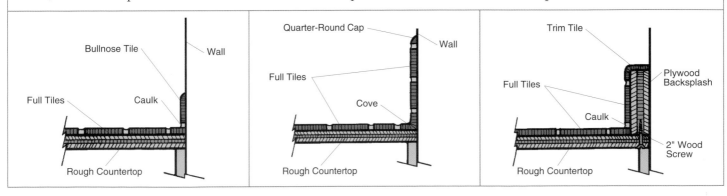

Laying the Tile

1 **Laying Edge Tiles.** Once the best layout has been determined, remove all the tiles that have been dry-laid. If sink caps or similar trim tiles will be used along exposed edges, mark a line along the edges on the rough countertop to allow for the width of the trim tiles. Then, align the guide strip with the pencil line and use it as the edge for laying the first row of full tiles. Using this method, the trim tiles will be laid after all the field tiles are in place.

If the edge will be finished with bullnose tiles, set them before the field tiles are set. First apply adhesive to the edge surface, butter the back of the apron tiles and set to line up with the field tiles. Then apply adhesive to the countertop and set the bullnose tile along the edge. It should overlap the top of the apron, creating a surface that is smooth and even.

If a wood edging is to be used, tack a straight 1x2 guide strip along the front of the countertop for positioning the first row of tiles in a straight line. Tack the guide strip so that it projects above the surface by the thickness of one tile.

Mark the centerline (starting point on the layout) for the first tile on the guide strip. Extend the line to the back of the countertop to aid in aligning tile courses.

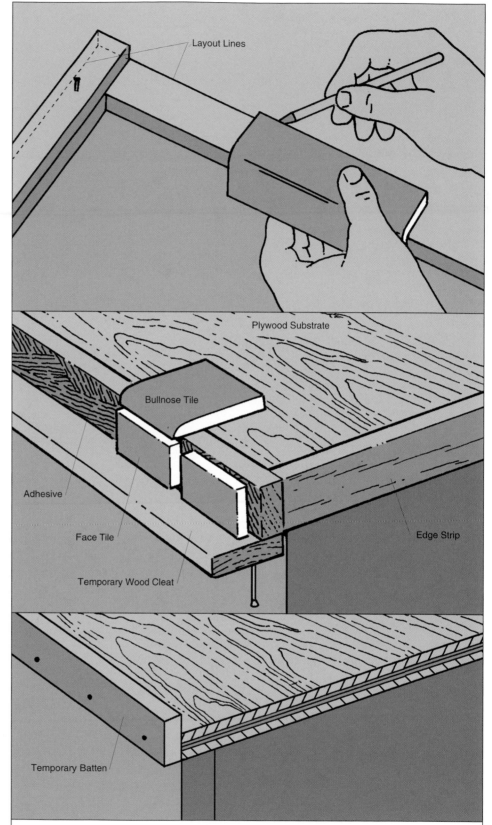

1 Mark the width of the trim tile on the front edge of the countertop; attach wood battens along the marked layout lines (top). If the edge will be finished with bullnose tiles, set them before the field tiles are set (middle). If whole tiles will be flush with the edges of the countertop, use battens at countertop edges to align tiles (bottom).

2 **Laying Whole Tiles.** With the starting point in mind, apply enough adhesive with a notched spreader to lay four or five tiles along the front edge. Lay the key tile first, butting it against the wood guide strip. Press it gently but firmly in place. Continue filling in tiles on either side of the key tile, using spacers, if necessary, until no more whole tiles will fit across the front.

Spread more adhesive and continue laying rows of full tiles, working back to the wall as far as possible without cutting any tiles. Check alignment frequently with a straightedge or framing square. Leave partial tiles and trim tiles until last, but scrape off any adhesive in the area where these will be placed before it dries. Once the full tiles are set, use a hammer and bedding block to bed them firmly in the adhesive. (See page 12.) Then check the surface with a straightedge or square to make sure it is level. If any tiles have "sunk" below surrounding ones, gently pry them out, apply more adhesive, and reset them.

3 **Cutting Partial Tiles.** Mark and cut partial tiles individually to make sure they fit the gap between the whole tiles and the wall or countertop edge. It is best to cut all the partial tiles at once, then install them. As each tile is cut, mark corresponding numbers on the back of the tile and on the rough top so the cut tiles do not get mixed up.

Once all the partial tiles are cut, spread adhesive along the work surface and press the tiles into place, with the cut edge facing the wall, sink cutout, or exposed end of the countertop. If the space is narrow, it is easier to apply adhesive to the back of the tile instead of the countertop. For more on cutting partial tiles. (See page 54.)

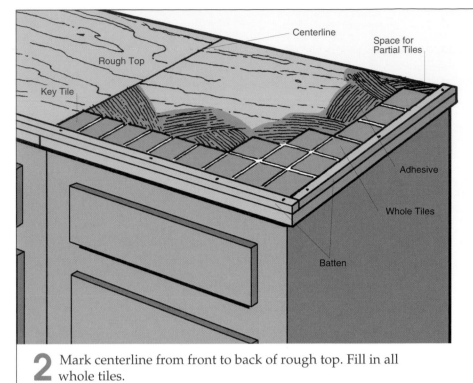

2 Mark centerline from front to back of rough top. Fill in all whole tiles.

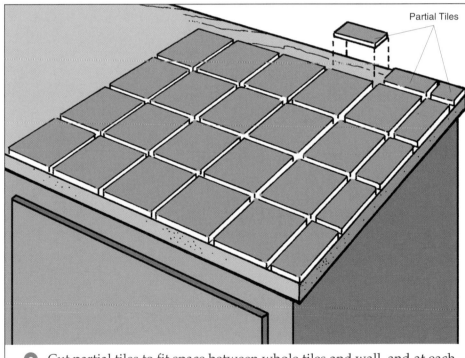

3 Cut partial tiles to fit space between whole tiles and wall, and at each end of countertop, if required. If space is narrow, butter back of tiles with adhesive and set into place.

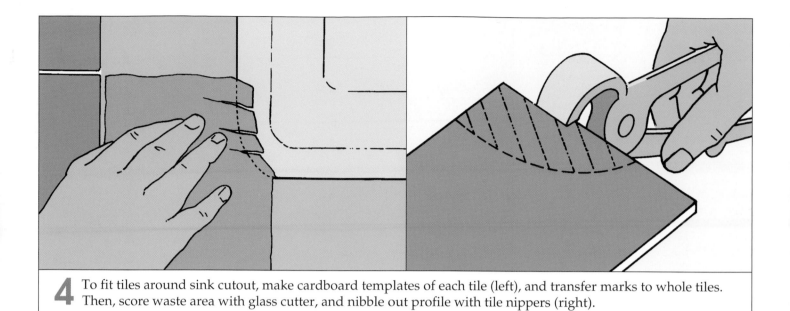

4 To fit tiles around sink cutout, make cardboard templates of each tile (left), and transfer marks to whole tiles. Then, score waste area with glass cutter, and nibble out profile with tile nippers (right).

4 Cutting Tiles Around a Sink. Square or rectangular sink basins usually have radius corners, which require curved cuts in tiles that fit against them; round or oval sinks require curved cuts all the way around. In either case, start by making tile-size templates from cardboard or paper. Hold the paper in place against the sink, then make a series of cuts in the edge with scissors or a sharp knife so that it can be folded in the shape of the curve.

Cut the curved shape out of the cardboard. Place the template on the tile, then mark and score the outline. Score a grid of lines on the waste side of the line and nibble away small pieces with nippers until the line is reached. If necessary, smooth the cut edge with a carborundum stone or file.

5 Adding Trim Tiles. If you have decided to use a wood edge instead of a tile trim, proceed to Step 6. Once the surface has been completely tiled with full and partial field tiles, remove the wood guide strips and finish the edges with trim tiles. Spread adhesive on the countertop and backsides of the tiles, then position trim tiles so that joints align with those of the field tiles. On L-shaped counters, begin at

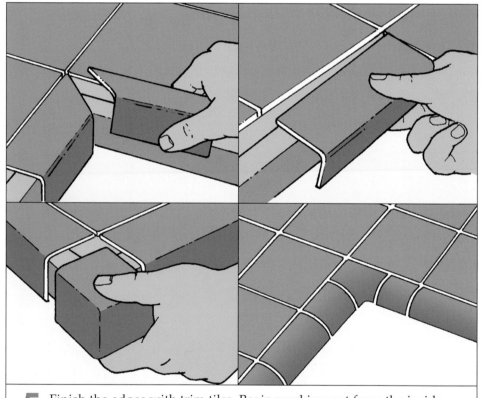

5 Finish the edges with trim tiles. Begin working out from the inside corner. Install the outside corner pieces last.

the inside corner with mitered tiles, or a special inside corner tile. If an inside corner tile is to be used, the first straight trim tiles on either side of it will need to be cut so grout joints of remaining straight pieces will align with those field tiles. To cut trim tiles, mark the cutline on the glazed side,

score deeply with a tile cutter and carefully nibble away the waste with tile nippers.

Fill in the straight trim tiles, working out from the inside corner. Finally, install the outside corner pieces.

6 **Wood Edging.** If you have chosen to use wood edging, install a filler strip to the underside of the countertop (if none already exists). Cut the wood edging to length, mitering the pieces where they meet at outside corners. Test for fit. The top edge of the strip should be flush with the tiled surface.

It is best to sand and finish the edging strips before they are

installed, to avoid damaging surrounding surfaces. Do not apply finish to the backside of the strip, as this might interfere with the adhesive bond.

Glue and screw the edging to the rough top. The strip is attached to the rough top with woodworker's glue or epoxy and countersunk wood screws. Cover the countersunk screwheads with dowel plugs of a matching or contrasting wood color. Or, the strip can be attached with countersunk finish nails. Fill nail holes with wood putty. When the tiles are grouted, also fill the gap between the molding and tile with grout (do not use silicone seal). Cover the wood strip with masking tape to protect it while grouting.

7 **Installing the Backsplash.** Set the backsplash tiles so they align with the countertop tiles. If tiling around electrical outlets, turn off the circuit breaker or unscrew the fuse to the outlet before the adhesive is applied around the outlet. If the outlet falls in the center of a tile, it is usually easier to split the tile in two, then to nibble out the opening profile in each half.

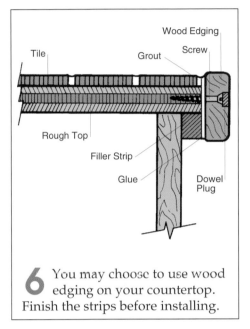

6 You may choose to use wood edging on your countertop. Finish the strips before installing.

Tile-Setting Tips

■ When tiling around a drop-in range or cooktop, leave a slight gap (about ¼ inch) between the tile and drop-in body of the unit to allow for expansion and contraction due to heating and cooling. Similarly, do not caulk or grout between the tiles and the range or cooktop surface.

■ If possible, use colored or dark grouts on kitchen countertops, as they are less likely to show stains than white grouts. Make sure the grout and sealer you use are recommended for use on food preparation surfaces; some contain mildewcides and other toxic chemicals.

■ On counter edges or overhangs, tile trim pieces, such as sink caps, always should be fully supported with a suitable backing, such as a wood filler or trim strip attached to the front edge of the rough top. (See page 56.)

5 Countertops

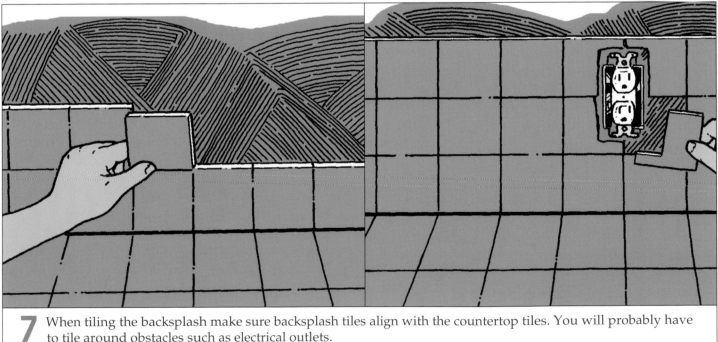

7 When tiling the backsplash make sure backsplash tiles align with the countertop tiles. You will probably have to tile around obstacles such as electrical outlets.

8 Applying the Grout. Allow the adhesive to set for an hour or two, then remove tile spacers, if they have been used. Use a damp cloth to clean any adhesive off the tile surface, then use a screwdriver or other pointed object to remove any excess adhesive in the joints between the tile. Allow the adhesive to cure for 24 hours before grouting. If unglazed tiles are used on the countertop, seal them before grouting. Use the sealant recommended by the tile manufacturer. Make sure the sealer has cured fully before applying the grout.

Mix the grout according to manufacturer's instructions and apply with a rubber float or squeegee, spreading the grout diagonally across the joints between the tile. Pack the grout firmly into every joint, being careful to eliminate any air bubbles.

When the grout becomes firm, use a damp sponge or rag to wipe off excess from the tile surface.

9 Finishing Up. Shape the grout joints with a striking tool (such as a toothbrush handle, spoon, or shaped stick). Clean off the tiles again and smooth the joints with a damp sponge. Allow a dry haze to form on the tile surface, then polish the tiles with a clean, damp cloth. In most cases, the grout will take several days to harden completely. Check manufacturer's recommendations.

10 Sealing. If the tile or grout joints require a sealer, apply it according to label directions. Make sure the wall is clean and completely dry. Starting in the corner farthest away from the door, apply a thin, even coat of sealer with a foam-rubber paint roller or sponge. Wipe off any excess to prevent discoloration of the tile. After the sealer has dried, apply a tile wax to bring out the beauty of the tile installation.

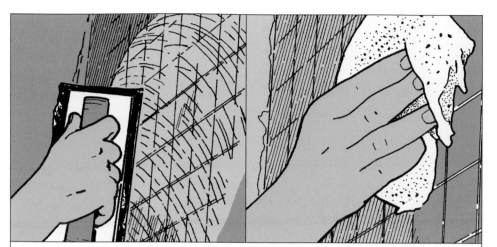

8 Apply the grout with a rubber float or squeegee, spreading it diagonally across the joints. When firm, use a damp sponge to wipe off excess.

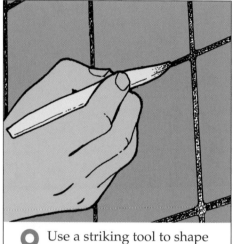

9 Use a striking tool to shape the grout joints.

10 Apply the sealer according to label instructions.

Caulking the Joint

Silicone rubber grout is used as caulking for edges around countertops, bathtubs, showers, etc. Once it has cured, the grout is resistant to staining, moisture, mildew, cracking and shrinking. It adheres tenaciously to ceramic tile, curing rapidly. It withstands exposure to hot cooking oils and free steam, as well as humid conditions. Since it is flexible, it is an excellent choice for surfaces that tend to move or shift slightly. Silicone grout is more expensive than the cement-based grouts and is available in white or clear.

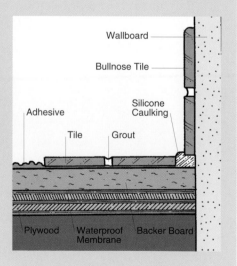

chapter 6

tubs & showers

Planning the Job

Tiling a tub surround or shower enclosure employs the same layout and tile-setting techniques used for walls. (See pages 39–54.) You should become familiar with these techniques before proceeding. If you are also tiling the shower floor, refer to pages 19–38 for basic tiling techniques. This section covers considerations specific to tiling tubs and showers. Most importantly is the need to provide a suitable waterproof backing on which to lay the tile.

Waterproofing

More than any other tiled surface in the house, a tub surround or shower enclosure must withstand direct contact with water and steam. For this reason, the tile installation and backing must be perfectly watertight. For maximum protection against water penetration, choose tiles with dense, non-porous body and durable glaze.

In addition, a water-resistant adhesive and grout (typically latex or acrylic thinsets) will have to be used to prevent water penetration between the tiles. Some grouts also contain additives that help prevent the growth of mildew, which can be a continuing problem in poorly ventilated bathrooms.

Even with water-resistant tiles, adhesives, and grouts, some moisture will eventually penetrate into the substrate. The backing also must be water resistant. Walls covered with conventional wallboard or plaster will not do. Remove these and replace them with water-resistant (green) wallboard, or a better choice, tile backer board. In many older installations, there will be some water damage to existing materials, anyway. Both backing materials require a special joint tape and mastic to make the panel joints and exposed edges waterproof. When installing green wallboard, leave a ¼-inch gap between the bottom of the panel and the lip of

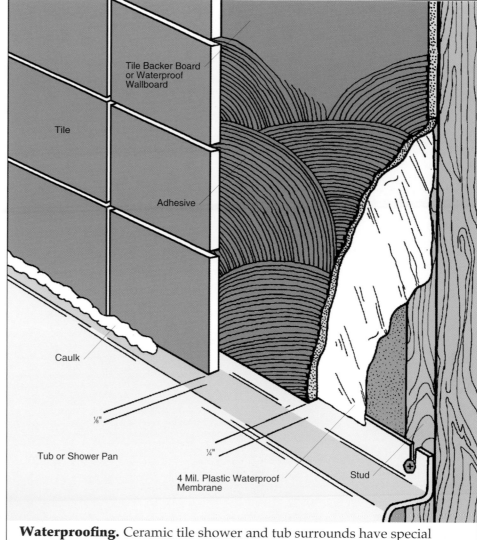

Waterproofing. Ceramic tile shower and tub surrounds have special waterproofing requirements. In modern installations, tile backer board is preferable to water-resistant (green) wallboard.

the tub. Install tile backer board all the way to the lip. Follow manufacturer's instructions for specific installation techniques.

While "green" wallboard and tile backer board will not be affected by water, some water may eventually penetrate through them. For this reason, building codes in most areas now require that a waterproof membrane—either 15-pound building felt (tar paper) or 4-mil polyethylene sheeting, be installed between the studs and backing material.

Because building codes and practices vary in different communities, check with your local building department for specific requirements.

Laying the Tile

1 Establishing Bottom Working Line. Ideally the job should start with a course of whole tiles around the tub rim or shower pan. When the horizontal lines for the three walls are established, allow for a ⅛-inch gap between the tub or shower pan and the first course of tiles. The gap will be filled with a mildew-resistant tub-and-tile caulk to allow for expansion and contraction between the two dissimilar materials. If the tub or shower pan is level to within ⅛ inch, locate the bottom horizontal line from the high point of the rim, measuring up ⅛ inch plus the width of one tile and one grout joint. The slight

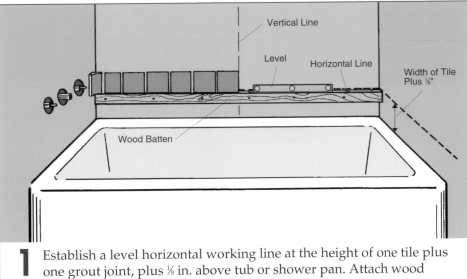

1 Establish a level horizontal working line at the height of one tile plus one grout joint, plus ⅛ in. above tub or shower pan. Attach wood batten so top edge is flush to working line. After filling in tiles above batten, remove it and fill in bottom row of tiles, cutting if necessary.

2 Starting at the bottom horizontal working line, measure up the wall at each corner to the height to be tiled. Strike a level line across the back wall; then extend the lines.

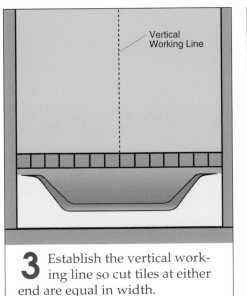

3 Establish the vertical working line so cut tiles at either end are equal in width.

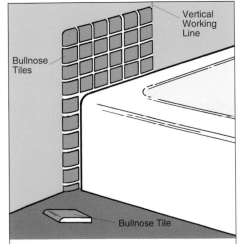

4 On end walls, adjust the vertical working line so grout joints align with front edge of tub. Finish off with a row of bullnose tiles.

variation in the gap between the rim and first course of tiles will not be noticed after it is caulked. If the tub or pan is more than ⅛ inch out of level, strike the horizontal line from the low end (again, measuring up ⅛ inch plus one tile and one grout joint). The first tile in the bottom course will be a whole tile; the rest will need to be taper-cut to maintain the required ⅛-inch gap. When the tiles are set to the horizontal lines, nail a batten to the working line to support the second course of tiles above the tub or pan, and install these first. The batten aids in alignment and prevents the tiles from slipping until the adhesive sets. Once it does, remove the batten and set the first course of taper-cut tiles.

2 Establishing Top Working Line. From the bottom horizontal working line, measure up the wall at each corner to the height to be tiled (a minimum of one tile above the shower head). Strike a level line across the back wall, then extend the lines across the two end walls, past the edge of the tub or pan.

3 Establishing Vertical Working Lines. The back wall of the shower stall or tub surround is the one that will be the most visible, so establish the vertical working lines on this wall first. As with tiled walls, adjust the vertical working line so cut tiles at each corner are equal in width and more than ½ tile wide. Figure the width of the inside-corner trim tiles, if used. Then establish the vertical lines on the end walls, in the same manner. The installation will look best if cut tiles on the inside corners of the end walls are equal in width to those on the back wall.

4 Extending the Tub Surround. If the walls extend beyond the sides of the tub but you do not want to tile the entire wall, extend the surround one tile beyond the front edge of the tub, and down to floor level. Usually, the last vertical row of field tiles are set flush to the front edge of the tub and bullnose tiles or trim is used to finish off the edges of the surround.

Extending the Enclosure

As with tubs, it usually is best to extend the tiled enclosure at least one tile past the front edge of the fiberglass shower pan or tiled shower threshold. The installation will look best if the grout joints and the top edge of the pan or threshold are in alignment. A cut tile may be needed at floor level.

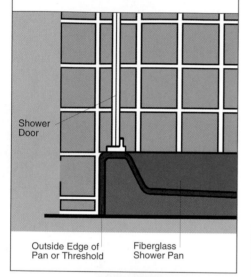

Shower Door

Outside Edge of Pan or Threshold

Fiberglass Shower Pan

Mounting Accessories

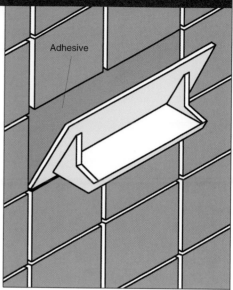

Adhesive

Soap Dishes. Many wall tiles come with matching accessories, such as ceramic soap dishes. Soap dishes are often sized in multiples of the tile dimensions. The soap dish itself will be mounted after the wall around its marked location is tiled. Position the ceramic soap dish to match the horizontal and vertical grout lines of surrounding field tiles, then mark its location on the wall. Some dishes have flanges that overlap surrounding tiles. Mark off the dimension of the part that will sit flush to the wall. If the soap dish will be recessed, cut any holes and install any required framing before tiling. Soap dishes attached directly to the wall generally require a stronger adhesive than the tile, so do not apply tile adhesive within the marked area for the accessory. An epoxy adhesive or special mastic-like adhesive will be used instead. Drying time may be several days, follow manufacturer's instructions. (See page 54.)

Grab Bars. Grab bars are installed before the tiling is done. Mount each end of the bar into studs behind the wallcovering or backing, then cut the tiles to fit around them. Most have escutcheons to hide the cutout.

Tile-Setting Tips

The tub and shower enclosure is a confined space so tile the back wall first, then fill in the sidewalls, and finally shower stub walls (partial front walls) and threshold (if the installation has these). Working this way will help prevent disturbing the tiles that have already been set.

■ Spread adhesive only on the surface to be tiled at the moment. Lay the first tile against the vertical working line where it meets the tub or pan, then work outward to each corner, allowing for grout lines between each tile. If tiles must be cut at either corner, cut the one preceding the vertical trim tiles (if used).

■ When applying the adhesive and setting the tile, complete one full wall before starting on the next. If the adhesive is applied to more than one wall before setting the tiles, the job will quickly become very messy.

■ To fit tiles around shower heads and faucets, split tile in half, then use tile nippers to cut the hole, or use a carbide-tipped hole saw chucked in a variable-speed drill. Caulk well before adding escutcheon plate.

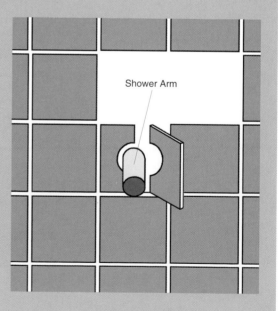

Shower Arm

other projects

Fireplaces

Whether you are building a new fireplace or you simply want to change the face of an existing one, ceramic tile makes an elegant, fireproof covering for a hearth or fireplace surround.

Tiling the Hearth

The term "hearth" generally applies to the horizontal surface immediately in front of the fireplace opening that protects the floor against heat, sparks and burning embers. A tiled hearth can be flush to the surrounding floor or raised above it. In new fireplace construction, the hearth can be built any distance to either side of the fireplace itself, to provide space for fireplace equipment and tools, wood, or fireside seating.

Tiling Existing Hearths. Ceramic tile can be set over an existing hearth of brick, concrete, or old tile, provided the surface is relatively smooth and flat. When dealing with a brick hearth or other rough surface, a thick bond coat of mortar or underlayment material that has been troweled onto the surface usually will fill in the mortar joints and provide a smooth base on which to lay the tile. First, grind down any high spots, then clean the surface thoroughly to remove any soot or dirt. Next, apply a smooth bond coat of mortar or underlayment, filling in any indents and irregularities. When the smooth bond coat dries, apply a second coat of mortar or thinset adhesive to set the tiles according to the manufacturer's instructions.

Enlarging a Hearth. An existing hearth can be extended to provide additional protection or to change its appearance. For instance, if the old hearth is covered with tile that you wish to save, but you cannot find matching tiles, use a contrasting tile border that will complement the old tile. Whether you are extending a raised hearth or a floor-level hearth, provide a suitable backing for the tile extension.

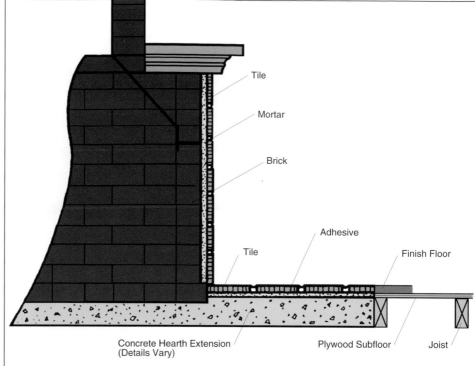

Tiling Existing Hearths. Typical cross section of tiled fireplace face with flush tiled hearth.

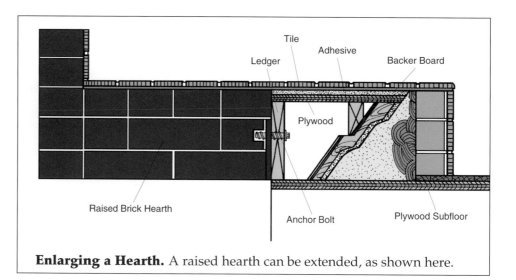

Enlarging a Hearth. A raised hearth can be extended, as shown here.

Floor-level hearths are usually slightly higher than the surrounding floor. First remove the finish flooring down to the plywood subfloor within the area to be tiled. Then build up the subfloor so the height of the new tile matches the old. Leave a ⅛-inch gap between the old hearth and extension, to provide for expansion. To extend a raised hearth, build a framework of 2x4s, either laid flat or on edge, as required to build up the extension to the height of the existing hearth.

Whether the hearth is flush or raised, provide a ⅛-inch gap between the tiled hearth and surrounding floor, and fill it with urethane or silicone caulk, to allow for seasonal movement between the dissimilar materials. Use a nonflammable dryset or latex-cement grout to finish off the installation.

Tiling the Face

Ceramic tile can add new life to an old, outdated fireplace surround and cover up chipped bricks or other damaged surfaces. The entire face can be covered, or tiles can be used in conjunction with other materials, such as an ornate wood mantel. The tiles used for the fireplace face do not have to be as thick or durable as those used for the hearth.

Because fireplaces come in many different designs and materials, it is not possible to give specific tiling instructions for every situation. On existing surrounds, use a heat-resistant epoxy to apply tile to wood, metal, wallboard, or existing ceramic tile. Use heat-resistant cement mortars on masonry surfaces or tile backer board. Ask a tile dealer which is best for you.

A common tiling project consists of a single row of decorative tiles around a prefabricated fireplace insert, with a wood mantel designed around it. In this case, the tiles are adhered directly to the existing (wallboard) wall around the fireplace opening; the wood mantel components are added after the tiles have been set. Adapt these tile-setting techniques to your specific project.

1 Set Horizontal Row. Tack a 1x2 batten across the top of the fireplace opening to support the horizontal row of tiles. Spread adhesive only on the wall area to be tiled. Set the horizontal row of tiles, spacing them so the end tiles align with the sides of the fireplace opening.

2 Remove Batten. When the adhesive has set (about 2 hours), remove the batten and set the tiles on both sides of the opening.

3 Apply Grout. Using a rubber float or squeegee apply grout to the tile joints. Remove the spacers (if used) and strike the grout joints.

4 Install Mantel or Trim. Add woodmantel pieces (if used). Quarter-round tile trim pieces also can be used.

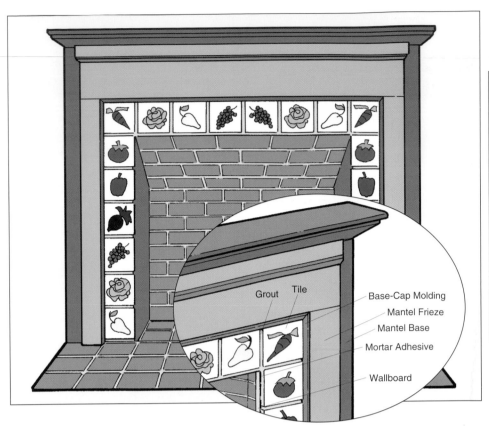

Grout Tile Base-Cap Molding
Mantel Frieze
Mantel Base
Mortar Adhesive
Wallboard

1 Spread adhesive on the wall area to be tiled.

2 When the adhesive has set, set the tiles on both sides.

3 Use a rubber float to apply grout to the tile joints.

4 Install mantel pieces or quarter-round trim tiles.

Woodstoves

Ceramic tile is also a good choice for hearths around woodstoves and freestanding fireplaces. The floor hearth can be flush or raised, round or square—a variety of design options exist. If you place the unit close to one or more walls, these also should be fireproofed. Again, local codes will dictate the size of the hearth, clearances, and the type of protective backing required.

Typically, the codes require minimum clearances for the stove or fireplace and combustible walls or floors. A combustible wall or floor is one that contains any flammable material. For example, wood frame walls and floors covered with a noncombustible surface, such as wallboard, tile, or plaster, are still considered combustible. Solid masonry walls (brick, stone, or concrete) are considered noncombustible, unless covered with a combustible material, such as wood paneling.

The clearances between the stove (front, sides, and rear) and combustible surfaces also will vary, depending on the type of stove or fireplace you have. Radiant stoves and fireplaces are those that enclose the fire with a single layer of metal. Examples are single-wall stoves and Franklin fireplaces. Minimum clearances recommended for these stoves by the National Fire Protection Association are shown in the following drawing.

Many modern woodstoves and freestanding fireplaces are of the "zero clearance" variety, which means they require little or no clearance between the firebox and combustible surfaces. However, these too should at least have a floor hearth to protect the floor in front of the firebox opening from errant sparks and embers.

There are several options for providing protection for combustible walls and floors, which enable reduced clearances between these and the

stove or fireplace. Typically a panel of ½-inch noncombustible insulation board or 24-gauge sheet metal spaced 1 inch away from the wall with noncombustible spacers is installed. In most cases, the tile alone will not provide sufficient protection for this purpose. In some communities, tile backer board can be used in lieu of insulation board.

As with hearths for conventional fireplaces, use a heavy, impact-resistant floor tile for the hearth. Thinner glazed wall tiles can be used on walls, if desired, although the hearth usually looks better when the same tile and trim is used for both walls and floor.

Laying the Tile. If the hearth to be built will extend up one or more walls behind the stove or fireplace, position any cut tiles for the floor hearth at the back corners. If tiles need to be cut at the sides of the hearth—at the floor, or wall—arrange for cuts wider than ½ tile and of equal width on both sides. The type of trim tiles used will depend on the height of the hearth's floor and thickness of any protective backing applied to the walls behind the tile. As with hearths for conventional fireplaces, use a heat-resistant epoxy or cement-based mortar and grout.

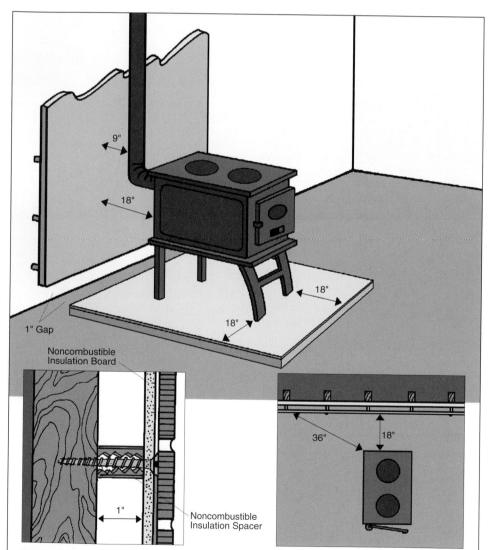

Woodstoves. Local building codes dictate clearances and materials used for installing a woodstove hearth. Specifications shown here are those recommended by National Fire Protection Agency.

Stairs

Indoors or out, tiled stairs or steps naturally call attention to themselves. A variety of tile treatments are possible. Stair design and construction varies considerably, and is beyond the scope of this book. Nevertheless, here are a few tips for tiling with them:

Tiled Risers. Indoors, long flights of stairs connecting one story to another often use a combination of wood and tile, typically hardwood treads and tiled risers. (Use 6 x 6-inch or 8 x 8-inch tile, depending on run and rise of stairs). Provide slight expansion gaps between the tiles and treads; and fill with flexible caulk.

Riser with Tiled Inlays. If constructing new stairs, consider installing oak or fir risers with spaced, decorative tiles inset into them. Make a tile-sized router template from ⅛-inch hardboard and rout recesses in the riser with a router fitted with a template guide. Use epoxy adhesive to set the tiles into the recesses.

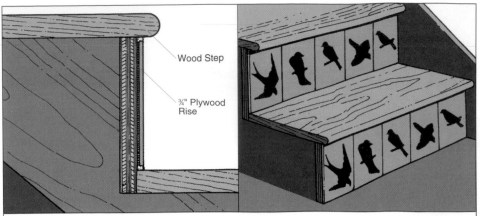

Wood Step

¾" Plywood Rise

Tiled Risers. Tiles are adhered to wood or plywood risers with an epoxy adhesive. Cover adjoining wood surfaces with masking tape when grouting.

Wood Step

Tile

Riser with Tiled Inlays. Use a router, template, and template guide to inset spaced tiles into wood risers.

Tips for Tiling Stairs

■ Tile the risers first, then the treads. Work from the top of the stairway down to the bottom so you are not forced to step on freshly laid tiles.

■ Slip-resistant floor tiles are a good choice for stair treads. Because the risers do not receive the foot traffic that the treads do, they can be covered with thinner decorative glazed wall tiles. Special slip-resistant stair nosings and frontings are available for further reducing the danger of accidental slips on the stairs. These consist of an aluminum channel with replaceable anti-slip PVC nosing inserts.

■ When calculating the dimensions of tread-riser ratios, do not forget to include the thickness of the tiles and any substrate materials. Plan the stairway so that the top tiled step will be flush with the adjoining floor, and all steps equal in width and height. Mark vertical layout lines on each tread and riser so that any cut tiles at each end will be more than ½ tile wide and equal in width. If the stairs or steps are reasonably level across their width, horizontal layout lines need not be established for each tread and riser.

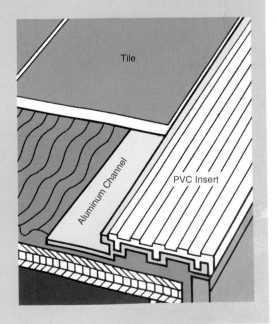

Tile

Aluminum Channel

PVC Insert

Tiles over Steps and Platforms. It is important to provide a suitable substrate. Use exterior-grade plywood (¾ inch minimum) to cover wood-frame steps and platforms; and provide adequate structural support to prevent flexing of the plywood. On steps or platforms over 16 inches deep, use two layers of ¾-inch plywood or one layer of plywood covered with tile backer board. Support treads on all edges. Adhere tiles to the plywood using an epoxy tile adhesive; use a latex-cement thinset adhesive over tile backer board.

Another option is to cover both the steps and risers with tile. If just a few wide steps are to be tiled, such as for a front entry or where floors of different levels meet, the front edge of the treads can be finished off with bullnose tiles. Large (8- or 12-inch square) unglazed quarry or paver tiles often are used for outdoor steps; while smaller (6- or 8-inch square) glazed floor tiles are used for interior steps. Place any cut tiles along the back edge of the tread and top edge of the riser.

Tile over Concrete Steps. Poured-concrete steps are relatively easy to tile and the resulting surface is beautiful and easy to maintain. Unglazed pavers and quarry tiles are popular choices for outdoor entry steps. In all cases, use a slip-resistant tile for the step treads; contrasting or decorative glazed tiles may be used for the risers. The concrete steps must be clean and free of major cracks or surface defects. Use a commercial driveway cleaner to remove grease and dirt and rinse thoroughly with clear water. Cracks and other defects can be repaired or patched as described for concrete floors; see pages 30–31. Also, if the steps have been painted, all loose or peeling paint must be removed, and the painted surface roughed up with a coarse (80–100 grit) silicon carbide or aluminum oxide sandpaper. Allow new concrete steps to cure for several weeks before applying tile. Use a latex-portland cement thinset adhesive recommended by the tile dealer.

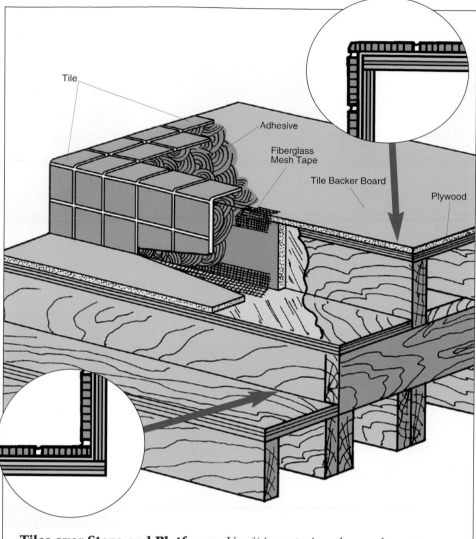

Tile
Adhesive
Fiberglass Mesh Tape
Tile Backer Board
Plywood

Tiles over Steps and Platforms. Use ¾-in. exterior plywood on steps and stairs less than 16 in. wide; use two layers of plywood, or plywood and backer board for wider steps and platforms.

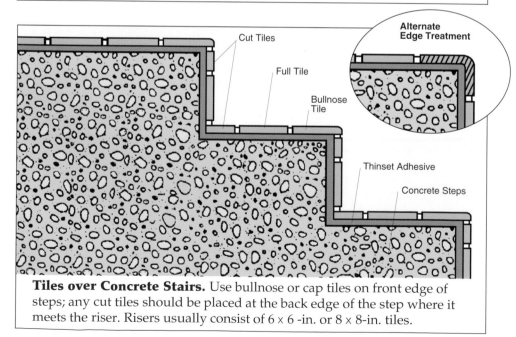

Cut Tiles
Full Tile
Bullnose Tile
Alternate Edge Treatment
Thinset Adhesive
Concrete Steps

Tiles over Concrete Stairs. Use bullnose or cap tiles on front edge of steps; any cut tiles should be placed at the back edge of the step where it meets the riser. Risers usually consist of 6 x 6 -in. or 8 x 8-in. tiles.

One of the reasons homeowners choose ceramic tile is that it is durable and easy to maintain. Even so, the tile and grout joints, which are especially susceptible to stains, do require periodic cleaning. Those dealing with an older installation may be faced not only with a cleaning job, but with cracked or broken tiles and deteriorating grout joints as well.

Cleaning. The day-to-day cleaning of ceramic tile requires only warm water and a sponge. Steel-wool pads will cause rust stains. A mild solution of white vinegar and water (or window cleaner) can remove light buildups of dirt, grease, soap scum, and water spots. For more stubborn dirt, grease, and stains use a strong solution of soap-free, all-purpose houschold cleaner or a commercial tile cleaner, and rinse thoroughly with clear water. Some tile cleaners also remove mildew stains from grout joints. Do not use harsh abrasives (scouring powders) on tile.

Stain Removal. Strong solutions of all-purpose household cleaners or commercial tile cleaners will remove most stains. Try these before resorting to the stain removal agents found in the chart above. Be sure to rinse household cleaners before applying stain removal agents.

Sealers. A clear sealer is usually applied to grout joints and unglazed tiles to protect the surface from stains and moisture penetration. As a part of tile maintenance, the sealer will have to be reapplied every year or two (as specified) in order to maintain that protection. If the tile and grout is becoming harder and harder to keep clean, it is time to apply more sealer.

Waxing and Buffing. Many tile waxes and buffing compounds are available for unglazed tile floors. Some tile waxes are colored to enhance the appearance of unglazed terra-cotta tiles or pavers. Consult a tile dealer for

Stain Removal Chart

Grease & fats (animal, cooking)	Concentrated solution of household cleaner
Tar, asphalt, oil, grease, oil paints, petroleum-based products	Charcoal lighter fluid followed by household cleaner, water rinse Outdoors: concrete/driveway cleaner
Ink, merthiolate, coffee, tea, blood, mustard, fruit juices, lipstick, colored dyes	Mild: 3% hydrogen peroxide solution Deep: full-strength household bleach
Nail polish	Wet: charcoal lighter fluid Dry: nail-polish remover
Liquid medicines, shellac	Denatured alcohol
Rust	Commercial rust remover, followed by household cleaner, rinse.
Chewing gum	Ice cube wrapped in cloth to chill gum so you can peel it off surface

Replacing Grout

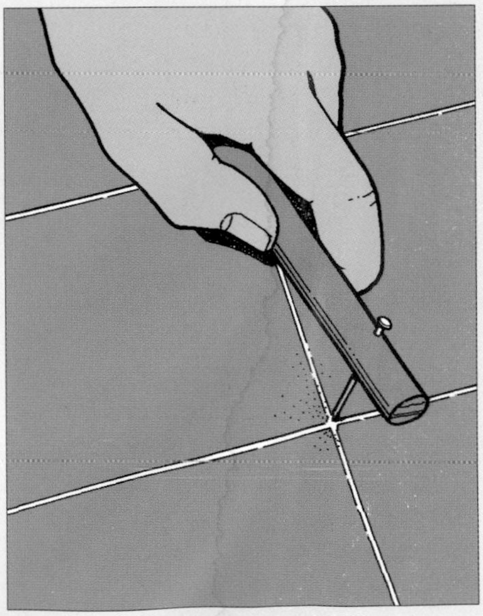

The easiest way to remove old grout is with a grout saw, available at tile dealers. For wide grout joints, a dry diamond blade or carborundum masonry blade in a circular saw can be used. (Wear safety goggles.) For narrow joints, a short length of hack-saw blade, or a nail stuck through a length of dowel can be used.

Once all the old grout is removed, wipe off the joints with a damp sponge and vacuum the debris off the floor and surrounding surfaces. Then apply new grout, following the instructions for floors. (See page 38.)

the best product. Generally, wax need not be applied each time the floor gets dull. After cleaning the floor with a soap-free floor cleaner and rinsing thoroughly with clear water, allow to dry and then buff out the existing wax to restore the shine. Small areas can be buffed by hand with a soft cloth, or a hand-held electric buffer. For large floors, rent a floor buffer.

Replacing Loose Tiles

Loose tiles most commonly occur on walls, especially in areas subjected to moisture, such as tub surrounds, shower enclosures and sink backsplashes. Loose wall tiles can be caused by several things, including a poorly prepared substrate, the wrong adhesive or backing, or cracked grout joints. As a result, moisture builds up behind the tile and breaks down the adhesive bond. In dry installations, excessive vibration, such as frequent slamming of doors, could be another possible source. The first step is to correct the problem; otherwise the tiles will loosen again after they have been replaced.

The following instructions also apply to loose floor tiles and countertop tiles.

1. Use a short length of hacksaw blade, an ice pick, or a beer-can opener to dig out the grout around the loose tiles. Carefully pry out each tile and scrape the dried adhesive off the wall and the back of the tile.

2. Allow the wall to dry thoroughly, then apply tile adhesive to the back of the tile and the wall, and press the tile in place. Clean off any excess adhesive. On walls, hold tile in place with masking tape and spacers, such as matchsticks or plastic tile spacers. Allow the adhesive to cure fully, then regrout. When the grout dries, apply a grout sealer.

Replacing Broken Tiles

1. Scrape away the grout surrounding the tile. Then, wearing safety glasses, use a hammer and cold chisel to break the tile into small pieces and chip it out. Avoid hard blows, and work from the center of the tile toward the edges to avoid damaging any surrounding tiles. Thin, glazed wall tiles will often break easier if you first score an X across the surface with a glass cutter.

2. Use a putty knife or wide-blade chisel to scrape the dried adhesive off the substrate. Spread adhesive on the back of a new tile and in the void created by the old one. Press the new tile in place, then grout and seal as described for replacing loose tiles.

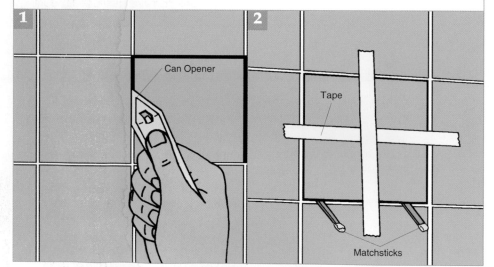

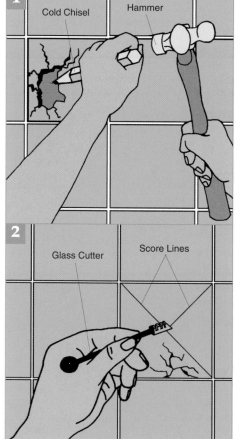

glossary

Backer board Cement-based panel with a fiberglass-reinforced coating; used as underlayment for tile. Also called cementitious backer units, or CBUs. Durock® and Wonderboard® are two popular brands.

Backsplash The tiled wall area behind a countertop, sink or stove.

Battens Thin wood strips used to support ceramic tile and ensure straight courses.

Beating block A block of wood covered with carpet or other protective material, used in conjunction with a hammer to bed tiles into adhesive.

Bisque The clay body of a tile, or the clay from which the tile is made.

Bond coat A thin layer of adhesive applied over the substrate.

Bridging Crossbrace supports between floor joists used to reinforce the floor.

Bullnose tile A trim tile with one rounded edge, used to finish off outside corners.

Buttering Applying adhesive to the back of a tile.

Carborundum stone A coarse-grit, silicone-carbide whetstone used to smooth cut edges of ceramic tile. Also called a Crystolon or India stone.

Cleats Blocks used to support wood braces or other members.

Cold chisel A heavy, blunt-edged chisel used in masonry work, typically for chipping or breaking up brick, stone, concrete, ceramic tile and other masonry materials.

Control joints Grooves cut into a concrete slab to confine cracking; cracks form along the joints rather than randomly across the slab.

Course A single row of tiles, usually runs horizontally.

Cove A trim or finishing tile that creates a smooth joint between adjacent walls, a wall and a floor, or other surfaces.

Cure The period of time that concrete, tile adhesive, or grout must be left in order for it to reach full strength.

Dry-set mortar A cement-based adhesive, so-called because it does not have to be kept constantly damp to cure.

Furring strip Narrow strips of wood attached to a surface to build it out. Provide nailing for underlayment panels.

Glass cutter A pencil-shaped metal tool, at one end of which is a wheel-shaped cutter used for scoring glass or glazed ceramic tile.

Grout A binder and filler applied in the joints between ceramic tile. Grouts may either be sanded (sand added) or unsanded.

Hearth A noncombustible horizontal surface in front of a fireplace; the hearth may be flush with the surrounding floor or raised above it.

Horizontal working lines Level, horizontal lines that serve as a guide for laying horizontal courses of tile on a wall or other vertical surface.

Isolation joint Flexible material inserted between two dissimilar floor or wall materials (concrete and wood, for example) to allow for different expansion rates.

Layout stick A straight, long, narrow stick marked in increments of tile widths and grout joints.

Lugs Nubs or projections formed into tile edges to maintain even spacing between tiles.

Mastic Common term used for organic-based adhesives.

Open time The amount of time adhesive can stay on a surface before it dries out and no longer forms an effective bond.

Organic adhesive A tile adhesive that contains volatile organic compounds or solvents; also referred to as mastic.

Plumb line A long string weighted at one end with a metal plumb bob, used to determine true vertical lines.

Porosity In tiling terms, the amount of water a ceramic tile will absorb.

Prime coat A sealer coat of adhesive or tile sealant that keeps the substrate from drawing moisture out of the tile adhesive.

Riser The vertical face of steps or stairs.

Rubber float A flat, rubber-faced tool used to apply grout.

Score To scratch or etch a cutline in a glazed tile, prior to cutting. The tile will snap or break along the scored line.

Sealer A liquid coating used to protect unglazed tiles and grout joints.

Shims Thin, wedge-shaped pieces of wood, such as cedar roof shingles, inserted in gaps between framing members to prevent movement or correct sagging.

Snap cutter A hand-operated tool used to make straight cuts in tiles.

Spacers Individually inserted lugs or plastic crosses of an even thickness, used to keep grout joints consistent between tiles.

Substrate The surface or underlayment to which tile is applied.

Step nosing An extruded aluminum strip with a vinyl insert, installed on the front edge of stair or step treads to provide traction and prevent slips.

Striking joints Shaping concave grout or mortar joints between tiles.

Stub walls Short or partial walls that form the opening in a shower enclosure

Thick-bed mortar A thick layer of mortar (more than ½ inch) that is used for leveling an uneven surface for tiling.

Thinset adhesives Any cement-based or organic adhesive applied in a thin layer (less than ½ inch) for setting tile.

Tile nipper Plier-type tool used to make irregular shaped cuts in tile.

Tread The horizontal face of a step or stair structure.

Trim tiles Specially formed tiles that are used to finish off inside or outside edges and corners of tile installations.

Underlayment Smooth panels of plywood, hardboard, or backer board used as a base for setting tile or other surfacing materials.

Vertical working lines Marked lines based on plumb, true, verticals; used as guides for laying vertical courses of tile on a wall.

Waterproof membrane A polyethylene film (usually 4 mil thick) or tar paper installed to prevent moisture condensation or penetration. Also called a vapor barrier.

index